STUDENT SELF-STUDY

SHOW WHAT YOU KNOW® ON THE

NASL

FOR GRADE 10

MATHEMATICS

PREPARATION FOR THE
WASHINGTON ASSESSMENT
OF STUDENT LEARNING

Published by:
Show What You Know® Publishing
A Division of Englefield & Associates, Inc.
P.O. Box 341348
Columbus, OH 43234-1348
Phone: 614-764-1211
www.showwhatyouknowpublishing.com
www.passthewasl.com

WASL Item Distribution information was obtained from the Washington Office of Superintendent of Public Instruction website, June 2005.

Printed in the United States of America
07 06 05   20 19 18 17 16 15 14 13 12 11 10 9 8 7 6 5 4 3 2 1

ISBN: 1-59230-142-8

ACKNOWLEDGEMENTS

Show What You Know® Publishing acknowledges the following for their efforts in making this assessment material available for Washington students, parents, and teachers.

Cindi Englefield, President/Publisher
Eloise Boehm-Sasala, Vice President/Managing Editor
Christine Filippetti, Project Editor
Jill Borish, Project Editor
Lainie Burke, Project Editor/Graphic Designer
Erin McDonald, Project Editor
Rob Ciccotelli, Project Editor
Jennifer Harney, Illustrator
Kathie Christian, Proofreader

ABOUT THE CONTRIBUTORS

The content of this book was written BY teachers FOR teachers and students and was designed specifically for the Washington Assessment of Student Learning (WASL) for Grade 10. Contributions to the Mathematics section of this book were also made by the educational publishing staff at Show What You Know® Publishing. Dr. Jolie S. Brams, a clinical child and family psychologist, is the contributing author of the Test Anxiety and Test-Taking Strategies chapters of this book. Without the contributions of these people, this book would not be possible.

Dear Student:

This *Show What You Know® on the WASL for Grade 10, Mathematics Student Self-Study Workbook* was created to give you practice in preparation for the Washington Assessment of Student Learning (WASL) in Mathematics.

The first two chapters in this workbook—Test Anxiety and Test-Taking Strategies—were written especially for tenth-grade students. Test Anxiety offers advice on how to overcome nervous feelings you may have about tests. The Test-Taking Strategies chapter includes helpful tips on how to answer questions correctly so you can succeed on the Mathematics section of the WASL.

The next chapter of this Student Self-Study Workbook will help you prepare for the Mathematics section of the WASL.

- The Mathematics chapter includes a Mathematics Practice Tutorial, two full-length Mathematics Assessments (Mathematics Assessment One—Session One and Session Two, Mathematics Assessment Two—Session One and Session Two), an Answer Key with answer analyses that will tell you why each answer is correct, and a Glossary of Mathematics Terms.

This Student Self-Study Workbook will help you become familiar with the look and feel of the Mathematics WASL and will provide a chance to practice your test-taking skills to show what you know.

Good luck on the WASL!

TABLE OF CONTENTS

Introduction iv

Test Anxiety 1

Test-Taking Strategies 11

Mathematics 27
   Introduction 27
   Understanding Grade Level Expectations 28
   Essential Academic Learning Requirements for Mathematics 29
   About the Mathematics WASL 43
      Item Distribution on the WASL for Grade 10 Mathematics 43
      Scoring 44
   Glossary of Mathematics Terms 51
   Glossary of Mathematics Illustrations 64
   Mathematics Formula Chart 68
   Directions for Mathematics Tutorial and Assessments 69
   Mathematics Practice Tutorial 74
   Mathematics Assessment One
      Mathematics Assessment One: Session One .159
      Mathematics Assessment One: Session One Skills Chart 172
      Mathematics Assessment One: Session One Answer Key 173
      Mathematics Assessment One: Session Two .176
      Mathematics Assessment One: Session Two Skills Chart 191
      Mathematics Assessment One: Session Two Answer Key 192
   Mathematics Assessment Two
      Mathematics Assessment Two: Session One .195
      Mathematics Assessment Two: Session One Skills Chart 208
      Mathematics Assessment Two: Session One Answer Key 209
      Mathematics Assessment Two: Session Two .212
      Mathematics Assessment Two: Session Two Skills Chart 226
      Mathematics Assessment Two: Session Two Answer Key 227
   Correlation Charts 231

TEST ANXIETY

WHAT IS TEST ANXIETY?

Test anxiety is a fancy term for feelings of worry and uneasiness that students have before or during a test. Almost everyone experiences some anxiety at one time or another. Experiencing feelings of anxiety before any challenge is a normal part of life. However, when worrying about tests becomes so intense it interferes with test taking, or if worrying causes students mental or physical distress, this is called test anxiety.

WHAT ARE THE SIGNS OF TEST ANXIETY?

Test anxiety is much more than feeling nervous. In fact, students will notice test anxiety in four different areas: thoughts, feelings, behaviors, and physical symptoms. No wonder test anxiety gets in the way of students doing or feeling well.

1. Thoughts

Students with test anxiety usually feel overwhelmed with negative thoughts about tests and about themselves. These thoughts interfere with the ability to study and to take tests. Usually, these bothersome thoughts fall into three categories:

- **Worrying about performance**—A student who worries may have thoughts such as, "I don't know anything. What's the matter with me? I should have studied more. My mind is blank; now I'll never get the answer. I can't remember a thing; this always happens to me. I knew this stuff yesterday and now I can't do anything."

- **Comparing oneself to others**—A student who compares performance might say, "I know everyone does better than I do. I'm going to be the last one to finish this. Why does everything come easier for everyone else? I don't know why I have to be different than others."

- **Thinking about possible negative consequences**—A student with negative thoughts would think, "If I don't do well on this test, my classmates will make fun of me. If I don't do well on the WASL Mathematics test, my guidance counselor will think less of me. I won't be able to go to my favorite college. My parents are going to be angry."

Many of us worry or have negative thoughts from time to time. However, students with test anxiety have no escape and feel this worry whenever they study or take tests.

2. Feelings

In addition to having negative thoughts, students with test anxiety are buried by negative feelings. Students with test anxiety often feel

- **Nervousness and anxiousness**—Students feel jittery or jumpy. Anxious feelings may not only disrupt test taking but may interfere with a student's life in other ways. Small obstacles, such as misplacing a book, forgetting an assignment, or having a mild disagreement with a friend, may easily upset students. They may become preoccupied with fear, may have poor self-esteem, and may feel that the weight of the world is on their shoulders. They seem to be waiting for "the next bad thing to happen."

- **Confusion and lack of focus**—Students with test anxiety have their minds in hundreds of anxious places. They find it difficult to focus on their work, which makes studying for tests even harder. Students with test anxiety also have difficulty concentrating in other areas. When they should be listening in class, their minds worry about poor grades and test scores. They jump to conclusions about the difficulty of an upcoming test. They find themselves fidgeting. They constantly interrupt themselves while studying, or they forget how to complete simple assignments. Anxiety can interfere with a student's ability to focus, study, and learn.

- **Anger and resentment**—Test anxiety can lead to irritable and angry feelings. Anxious students are defensive when communicating with others. They become overwhelmed by negative thoughts and feel they are not good enough. Test anxiety also makes students feel "trapped" and as though they have no escape from school or tests. Students who feel there is no way out may get angry; they may resent the situation. They feel jealous of people they believe find school easier. They are angry at the demands placed on them. The more angry and resentful students become, the more isolated and alone they feel. This only leads to further anxiety and increases difficulties in their lives.

- **Depression**—Anxiety and stress can lead to depression. Depression sometimes comes from "learned helplessness." When people feel they can never reach a goal and that they are never good enough to do anything, they tend to give up. Students who are overly anxious may get depressed. They lose interest in activities because they feel preoccupied with their worries about tests and school. It might seem as though they have no time or energy for anything. Some students with test anxiety give up on themselves completely, believing if they cannot do well in school (even though this may not be true), then why bother with anything?

Not all students with test anxiety have these feelings. However, if you or anyone you know seems to be overwhelmed by school, feels negative most of the time, or feels hopeless about school work (test taking included), you should look to a responsible adult for some guidance.

3. Behavior

Students with test anxiety often engage in behavior that gets in the way of doing well. When students have negative thoughts and feelings about tests, they participate in counterproductive behavior. In other words, they do things that are the opposite of helpful. Some students avoid tests altogether. Other students give up. Other students become rude and sarcastic, making fun of school, tests, and anything to do with learning. This is their way of saying, "We don't care." The truth is, they feel anxious and frustrated. Their negative behaviors are the result of thoughts and feelings that get in the way of their studying and test taking.

4. Physical Symptoms

All types of anxiety, especially test anxiety, can lead to very uncomfortable physical symptoms. Thoughts control the ways in which our bodies react, and this is certainly true when students are worried about test taking. Students with test anxiety may experience the following physical symptoms at one time or another:

- sweaty palms
- stomach pains
- "butterflies" in the stomach
- difficulty breathing
- feelings of dizziness or nausea

- headaches
- dry mouth
- difficulty sleeping, especially before a test
- decrease or increase in appetite

Test anxiety causes real physical symptoms. These symptoms are not made up or only in your head. The mind and body work together when stressed, and students can develop uncomfortable physical problems when they are anxious, especially when facing a major challenge like the WASL.

THE TEST ANXIETY CYCLE

Have you ever heard the statement "one thing leads to another?" Oftentimes, when we think of that statement, we imagine Event A causes Event B, which leads to Event C. For example, being rude to your younger brother leads to an argument, which leads to upset parents, which leads to some type of punishment, like grounding. Unfortunately, in life, especially regarding test anxiety, the situation is more complicated. Although one thing does lead to another, each part of the equation makes everything else worse, and the cycle just goes on and on.

Let's think back again to teasing your younger brother. You tease your younger brother and he gets upset. The two of you start arguing and your parents become involved. Eventually, you get grounded. Sounds simple? It might get more complicated. When you are grounded, you might become irritable and angry. This causes you to tease your little brother more. He tells your parents, and you are punished again. This makes you even angrier, and now you don't just tease your little brother, you hide his favorite toy. This really angers your parents, who now do not let you go to a school activity. That upsets you so much you leave the house and create trouble for yourself. One thing feeds the next. Well, the same pattern happens in the test anxiety cycle.

Look at the following diagram.

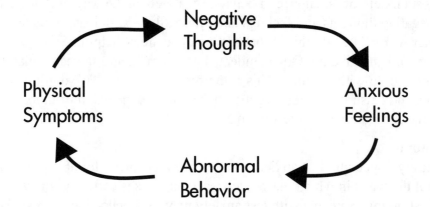

As you can see, the four parts of this diagram include the thoughts, feelings, behavior, and physical symptoms discussed earlier. When a student has test anxiety, each area makes the others worse. The cycle continues on and on. Here's an example:

Let's start off with some symptoms of negative thinking. Some students might say to themselves, "I'll never be able to pass the WASL Mathematics test!" This leads to feelings of frustration and anxiety. Because the student has these negative thoughts and feelings, his or her behavior changes. The student avoids tests and studying because they are nerve racking. Physical symptoms develop, such as the heart racing or the palms sweating. Negative thoughts then continue, "Look how terrible I feel; this is more proof I can't do well." The student becomes more irritable, even depressed. This affects behavioral symptoms again, making the student either more likely to avoid tests or perhaps not care about tests. The cycle goes on and on and on.

IS TEST ANXIETY EVER GOOD?

Believe it or not, a little worrying can go a long way! Too much test anxiety gets in the way of doing one's best, but students with no anxiety may also do poorly. Studies have shown that an average amount of anxiety can help people focus on tasks and challenges. This focus helps them use their skills when needed. Think about a sporting event. Whether a coach is preparing an individual ice skater for a competition or is preparing the football team for the Friday night game, getting each athlete "psyched up" can lead to a successful performance. A coach or trainer does not want to overwhelm the athlete. However, the coach wants to sharpen the senses and encourage energetic feelings and positive motivation. Some schools have a team dinner the night before a competition. This dinner provides some pleasant entertainment, but it also focuses everyone on the responsibilities they will have the next day.

Consider the graph below. You can see that too little test anxiety does not result in good test scores. As students become more concerned about tests, they tend to do better. But wait! What happens when too much anxiety is put into the equation? At that point, student performance decreases remarkably. When anxiety reaches a peak, students become frustrated and flustered. Their minds tend to blank out, they develop physical symptoms, they cannot focus, and they also behave in ways that interfere with their performance on tests.

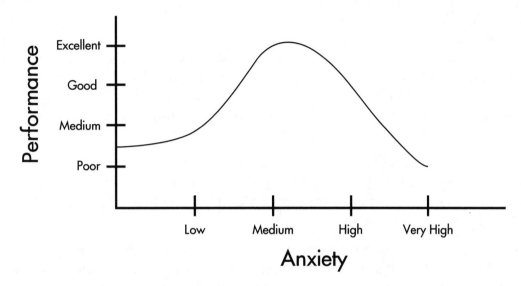

An important key to successful test taking is to get yourself in the "right mood" about taking a test. Looking at a test as a challenge and looking forward to meeting that challenge, regardless of the end result, give you a positive and healthy attitude. You will feel excited, motivated, and maybe a little nervous, but certainly ready to face the WASL.

HOW DO I TACKLE TEST ANXIETY?

Although test anxiety is an uncomfortable and frustrating feeling, the good news is you can win the battle over test anxiety! Conquering test anxiety will not be accomplished by luck or magic, but it can be done by students of all ages in a relatively short period of time. If you can learn to master test anxiety at this point in your life, you will be on the road to successfully facing many other challenges you will encounter.

1. Change the Way You Think

Whether you realize it or not, your thoughts—good and bad—influence your life. The way we think is related to how we feel about ourselves, how we get along with other people, and how well we do in school, especially when taking tests.

• *Positive Thinking Can Block Out Negative Thinking*—It is impossible to think two opposite thoughts at the same time. You may have one idea and then think about another, but one is always going to "win" over the other. When you practice positive thinking, you are replacing negative thoughts with positive ones. The more you are able to think positive thoughts, the less you will be troubled by negative ones.

- *The Soda Pop Test*—It's just as easy to have positive thoughts as negative ones. Everyone has heard the saying, "There is more than one side to any story." Just as there are two opinions on any given subject, there is generally more than one way to look at almost every situation in life. Some ways are more helpful than others.

Think about a can of soda pop. Draw a line down the middle of a blank piece of paper. On one side, put the heading, "All the bad things about this can of soda pop." On the other side, put another heading, "All the good things about this can of soda pop." Now, write appropriate descriptions or comments under each heading. For example, you could write, "This can of soda pop is a lot smaller than a two-liter bottle," which is negative thinking. Or, you could write, "This can of soda pop is just the right size to stay cold and fizzy until I finish it." It's easy to look at the soda-pop can and think bad thoughts. But you are also able to come up with many good things. If you spent all your time focusing on the negative aspects, you might believe the can of soda pop is bad. It is better to look at the positive side of things.

Part of successful test taking has to do with how you look at tests. With the can of pop, you could choose to think negatively, or you could have positive thoughts. The same holds true for tests. You can look at a test as a scary or miserable experience, or you can look at a test as just one of many challenges you will face in your life.

Counselors have known for years that people who are worried or anxious can become happier when thinking positive thoughts. Even when situations are scary, such as going to the dentist or having a medical test, "positive imagery" is very helpful. Positive imagery simply means focusing on good thoughts to replace anxious thoughts.

You can replace negative thoughts with positive ones through practice. Believe it or not, it really works!

- *Thoughts of Success*—Thinking "I can do it" thoughts chases away ideas of failure. Times that you were successful, such as when you did well in a sports event or figured out a complicated math question, are good things to think about. Telling yourself you have been successful in the past and can now master the Mathematics section of the WASL will replace thoughts that might otherwise cause anxiety.

- *Relaxing Thoughts*—Some people find that thinking calming or relaxing thoughts is helpful. Picturing a time in which you felt comfortable and happy can lessen your anxious feelings. Imagining a time when you visited the ocean, climbed a tree, or attended a concert can help you distract your mind from negative thoughts and focus on times when you were relaxed and felt happy and positive.

- *All-or-Nothing Thinking*—Nothing is ever as simple as it seems. Sometimes we convince ourselves something is going to be completely "awful" or "wonderful," but it rarely turns out that way.

No test is "completely awful" or "completely perfect." Tests are going to have easy questions and hard questions, and you are going to have good test days and bad test days. The more you set up expectations that are all positive or negative, the more stressful the situation becomes. Accepting that nothing is totally good or bad, fun or boring, or easy or hard will reduce your anxiety and help you set reasonable expectations about tests. When you think about tests, try not to think about them as the road to academic success or a pit of failure. Instead, realize that all challenges have both good and bad elements, and that you have to take everything in stride.

- *Making "Should" Statements*—Making "should" statements sets students up for failure. Sure, it is important to try your best, to study hard, and to make a reasonable effort on the WASL; it may even be good to take an extra study session, try another practice test, or ask a teacher or tutor for advice and suggestions. It is also a good idea to use a book such as this one to help you do your best and show what you know. However, there is a big difference between doing your "reasonable best" and living your life with constant worries and put-downs. Students who constantly tell themselves "I should" and berate themselves for not having done everything possible only increase their levels of anxiety.

Go back to the test anxiety cycle. Suppose your thoughts are, "I should have stayed up an extra hour and studied," or "I should have reviewed those geometry formulas." The more you think these thoughts, the more anxious you get. The more anxious you get, the worse you feel. Again, the cycle goes on and on.

One part of maturing is learning to balance your life. Life is happiest when you find a good balance between being a lazy do-nothing and being a perfectionist. While we all know laziness gets us nowhere, being a perfectionist may actually paralyze your future chances of success because you will eventually fear facing any new challenges. Remember, failure does not mean real failure; it just means being imperfect. Preventing perfectionism begins by saying "no" to unreasonable thoughts and "should" statements. "Should" statements place high demands on a student and only lead to frustration and feelings of failure, shame, and anxiety.

Students who always think about what they "should" do often exhaust themselves by doing too much and worrying excessively. Exhaustion is another factor that leads to poor test-taking results.

Breaking the "should" habit means replacing "should" statements with positive comments about what you have accomplished and what you hope to reasonably accomplish in the future. For example, instead of saying, "I shouldn't have gone to the football game," or "I should have stayed home and studied," say, "I studied for two hours before the football game, and then I had a good time. Two hours was plenty of time to study for a geometry quiz. I need to have time for friends as well as studying. I concentrated while studying, and I think I did a good job. Even if I don't get a perfect score on the geometry quiz, I know I will do pretty well, and I gave myself the opportunity to do my best."

2. Control Physical Symptoms

Changing your physical response to stress can help break the test anxiety cycle. Relaxing is difficult when facing a major challenge such as the WASL, but there are many proven techniques that can help you calm down.

- *Relax the Morning of the Test*—Try to allow yourself to relax the morning of the test. Engaging in some mild exercise, such as taking a walk, will relieve a lot of your physical stress. Some students may find that a workout the night before an exam makes them feel more relaxed and helps them sleep well. This is probably because the exercise distracts the student from the upcoming test. Also, intense exercise releases chemicals in the brain that cause you to feel calmer and happier. It may only take a quick walk around the block to help you relax and get your mind off your problems.

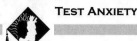
- *Listen to Music*—Listening to music in the morning before a test may also be helpful for students. It probably doesn't matter what kind of music you listen to as long as it makes you feel good about yourself, confident, and relaxed.

- *Relaxation Exercises*—Relaxation exercises are helpful to many students. Stress causes many physical changes in the body, including tenseness in all muscle groups, increased heart rate, and other physical symptoms. Learning simple exercises to feel less tense can also help break the test anxiety cycle.

Most exercises include tightening and releasing tension in your body as well as deep breathing. The purpose of all of these exercises is to distract you from the anxiety of an upcoming test and to allow your body to feel more loose and relaxed. These exercises can be completed while sitting at your desk, taking a test, or studying.

Try this simple relaxation exercise the next time you are tense. Sit upright in your chair, but allow yourself to be comfortable. Close your eyes and take four deep breaths in and out. When you get to the fourth breath, start breathing quietly but remain focused on your breathing. Start increasing the tension in your feet by squeezing your toes together tightly and then slowly releasing the pressure. Feel how relaxed your toes are feeling? Now tighten and release other muscle groups. Go from your legs to your stomach, to your shoulders, to your hands, and finally to your forehead. Squeeze and tighten your muscles and then relax them, all while focusing on your breathing. Once you practice this strategy, you might feel more relaxed in a matter of seconds. This would be a good strategy to use when you feel yourself becoming unfocused and anxious during tests.

PREPARE FOR THE MATHEMATICS SECTION OF THE WASL AND CHANGE THE WAY YOU BEHAVE

Preparation always reduces anxiety. Taking the WASL Mathematics test seriously, trying to do well on practice tests, and making an effort in all your classes will help you feel more confident and relaxed about the WASL. Learning test-taking strategies can also give you a feeling of power and control over the test. No feeling is worse than realizing you are not prepared. Going into a test without ever having reviewed the WASL Mathematics material, looked at test-taking strategies, or concentrated on your school work is very much like jumping out of an airplane without a parachute. You would be foolish if you were not panicked. Looking at the WASL Mathematics section as just one more reason to take school seriously will help your grades, attitude, and success on the test.

1. Use Mental Preparation

Before the test, imagine in step-by-step detail how you will perform well and obtain a positive result. Several days before the test, think through the day of the test; repeat this as many times as you need. Imagine getting up in the morning, taking a nice shower, getting dressed in comfortable clothes, and listening to music on your way to school. Think about sitting in the testing room with a confident expression on your face. Imagine yourself remembering all of the strategies you read about in this book and learned in your classroom. Go through an imaginary test, step by step, practicing what you will do if you encounter a difficult question. You should also repeat the positive thoughts that should go through your head during the test. Preparation like this is key for reducing anxiety, as you already feel you have taken the test prior to ever having stepped into that testing room!

2. Don't Feel Alone

People feel more anxious when they feel alone and separate from others. Have you ever worried about a problem in your family or something going wrong at school? Things seem much worse when you are alone, but when you talk to someone who cares about you, you will find your problems soon seem less worrisome. Talk to your friends, parents, and teachers about your feelings. You will be surprised at the support you receive. Everyone has anxious feelings about tests. Having others understand your anxious feelings will help you accept yourself even more. Other people in your life can also give you suggestions about tests and can also help you put the WASL Mathematics and other tests in perspective.

3. Congratulate Yourself During the Test

Students with test anxiety spend a lot of time putting themselves down. They have never learned to say good things about themselves or to congratulate themselves on successes. As you go through the WASL Mathematics, try to find ways to mentally pat yourself on the back. If you find yourself successfully completing an extended-response question, tell yourself you did a good job. When you finish reading a Mathematics test item and feel you understand the information fairly well, remind yourself you are doing a good job in completing the WASL Mathematics. Paying attention to your successes, and not focusing on your failures, can greatly reduce test anxiety.

TEST-TAKING STRATEGIES

UNDERSTAND THE TYPES OF POSSIBLE QUESTIONS ON THE MATHEMATICS SECTION OF THE WASL

In preparing for the Mathematics section of the WASL, you will need to think about the various types of questions you might be asked, but you also must think about and practice the different types of answers that will be required.

Remember being five years old? It was your grandmother's birthday, so you drew her a picture of a birthday cake and a flower. It was cute, but that was the only way you could give her a gift. You didn't have any money, and you didn't have a lot of experience in making gifts or sharing birthday wishes. Now, you have lots of choices as to how you can wish her "Happy Birthday."

As a high school student, you have been exposed to many ways to express a mathematical answer or concept, and the Mathematics section of the WASL expects you to be able to show what you know in more than one way. So, as you work through mathematical problems in school, think about different ways to illustrate your answers and describe your work.

On the Mathematics sections of the WASL, you could be asked to do the following:

• Give a brief explanation of why you chose a particular multiple-choice answer. • Use a figure or diagram to explain an answer. • Show the correct equation that resulted in your answer. • Use a few sentences to clearly describe your answer. • Create a table or graph.	• Organize information to find an answer. • Use equations, graphs, diagrams, tables, or words to prove or verify an answer. • Use set aside spaces in the test booklet to show multiple steps or answer multiple parts of a question. • Use appropriate mathematical vocabulary words in answers.

Mathematics is a language, and learning how to speak in that language is not an easy task. That is why practicing speaking like a mathematician can go a long way toward success on the WASL.

USE A CHECKLIST TO THINK THROUGH PROBLEMS

Do you remember elementary school? Remember your teacher giving you checklists to help you do your best? Well, checklists are still helpful tools, especially on the Mathematics WASL.

Even though much of the mathematics that you are learning is more complicated than what you were taught as a child, having a set pattern of reviewing your work can lead to a better result on this test.

As you tackle mathematics questions, get in the habit of asking yourself these questions:

> ☑ Did I read the problem carefully? Misreading the problem will certainly lead to a poor result.
>
> ☑ What solution does the problem require? Does it ask for a single number, or for something else?
>
> ☑ What information can I use to solve the problem? Are there charts, diagrams, or other information that I can use to solve a problem or explain a process?
>
> ☑ Did I answer the problem in the manner it was asked? Did I show my work or respond with a requested equation or figure? For example, did I draw a diagram if I was asked to do so?
>
> ☑ Did I use all the tools I have to answer the problem? Could a calculator have been helpful? Are there other ways that I could explain my answer, such as adding a sentence or diagram?
>
> ☑ Did I write legibly? Can I read both my written numbers and words? Are my drawings understandable?
>
> ☑ Did I use mathematical vocabulary and language whenever I could?
>
> ☑ Does my answer make sense? Based on my knowledge of mathematics, is this a reasonable answer?

KNOW YOUR TOOLS

On the Mathematics section of the WASL, you may use a calculator in Session One of the test to find some answers. These questions test your ability to understand the process of finding a correct answer, not your skills at quickly performing routine calculations without help. Unfortunately, using a calculator won't be helpful if you don't know how to quickly and accurately use a calculator, and may actually cause you to arrive at the wrong answer.

Using a calculator takes practice. When you first learned a computer keyboard, you were slow and made many mistakes. If you rely on your parents or friends to type for you, you probably haven't improved your keyboarding skills very much since elementary school. If you had to type your answers on the WASL, it would take you a long time, and you would have many mistakes. The same amount of practice is needed for a calculator in order for it to be helpful to you on the Mathematics section of the WASL. Students who avoid using a calculator except when absolutely necessary will not benefit from using one when taking the WASL. So, if you are not comfortable with a calculator, practice! It will not only help you on the test, but you will find this skill valuable in jobs and for solving problems in your everyday life.

KNOW YOUR VOCABULARY

When most students think of vocabulary words, they think of reading and writing, not mathematics. In fact, having a good understanding of mathematical words will be as helpful to you on the WASL as having a comprehensive vocabulary in writing and speaking.

You have been taught many important mathematical terms beginning in elementary school, and many of them will be in the questions and answers on the Mathematics section of the WASL. A good strategy when preparing for this test is to make a mathematics vocabulary list with correct definitions and examples. Take a peek at some of your old textbooks and the ones you are using now. You could even go to the library and find some middle school textbooks or other mathematics books. Every day, find one or two words and get to know them well! In a short time, you will be surprised to find that you have mastered a fairly large number of mathematical concepts.

In this book, you will find a Mathematics Glossary and a Glossary of Illustrations that will provide you with some important mathematical definitions and concepts. There also may be other terms and concepts that you should review. By studying words and phrases such as "vertex," "coordinates," "inverse property," or "function," you will find it easier to express yourself in mathematical terms. For example, regarding the term "associative property," you might note:

Associative Property: This means the grouping of numbers does not affect the sum or product of the numbers. An example would be: $(3 + 4) + 5 = 3 + (4 + 5)$ or $(6 \times 10) \times 3 = 6 \times (10 \times 3)$.

You will remember information better by

> • Writing the information more than once
> • Using examples
> • Discussing your examples with a parent, friend, or teacher

DON'T FORGET THOSE FORMULAS!

Few students like to memorize, but those who memorize certain facts and formulas have better success on the Mathematics WASL. Some multiple-choice items will ask you to identify a correct formula for solving a problem. Many enhanced multiple-choice, short-answer, and extended-response items will require you to show your work and include the formula you used to solve the problem.

There are certain facts and formulas that you are expected to have memorized. Your teacher, in preparation for the WASL, will review most of these important formulas. Just as with familiarizing yourself with mathematical vocabulary words, you should memorize formulas and facts to help you do your best. Keep in mind that memorization works best when you use the information over and over again in your school work.

Examples of what you should know include the following:

> • Calculating the volume of a prism and cylinder
> • Converting units of measurement, such as meters into centimeters
> • Simplifing expressions
> • Finding the equation of a line
> • Solving for a particular variable

MULTIPLE-CHOICE QUESTIONS

USE "CODES" TO MAKE BETTER GUESSES

You might find it helpful to use "codes" to rate multiple-choice answers. Using your pencil in the test booklet, you can mark the following codes beside each multiple-choice response to see which is the best choice. An example of a code used by a tenth-grade student is given below.

(+) Put a "plus sign" by an answer choice if you are not sure if it is correct, but you think it might be correct;

(?) Put a "question mark" by an answer choice if you are not sure if it is the correct answer, but you don't want to rule it out completely;

(-) Put a "minus sign" by an answer choice if you are sure it is the wrong answer. (Then choose from the other answers to make an educated guess.)

Remember, it is fine to write in your test booklet. The space in the booklet is yours to use to help you do better on the WASL. You will not have points counted off for using this coding system or creating your own system to help you on multiple-choice questions.

ANSWER EVERY QUESTION

It is very important to answer as many multiple-choice questions as possible, even if you make an educated guess. On multiple-choice questions, you have a one in four chance of getting a question right, even if you just close your eyes and guess! This means that for every four questions you guess, the odds are you will get about one (25%) of the answers right. Guessing alone is not going to make you a star on the WASL, but leaving multiple-choice questions blank is not going to help you either.

TAKE ADVANTAGE OF "CHANCE"

On the Mathematics section of the WASL, multiple-choice questions carry less weight than short-answer or extended-response items, but increasing your success on multiple-choice answers should increase your test-taking success. It is very important to answer as many multiple-choice questions as possible, even if you make a well thought out guess, because luck is with you! If you can eliminate even one possible answer, your chances of success are now even better! The best way to improve your chances on multiple-choice questions is to use strategies such as using codes and power guessing that are described in this chapter. Learning how to improve your chances by using educated guessing is not cheating! In fact, you probably use this strategy outside of the classroom and don't even think about it. Imagine you have misplaced your favorite CD, and you want to find it before you leave for your friend's house. There are many possible places that it could be, but you use your common sense to eliminate some possibilities, thereby saving time searching and increasing your chances of finding it in time. For example, it might be possible that you left it in your sister's room, but you remember, "That isn't likely because her CD player has been broken for a month." That leaves you one less place to look, and more chances for success.

UNDERSTAND MULTIPLE-CHOICE QUESTIONS AND ANSWER CHOICES

Each multiple-choice question will have four possible answers that follow either a question or a statement. For example, you might be asked, "The new school auditorium is 400 feet long and 200 feet wide, and the stage makes up 25% of the space. How much room is there for a set to be built?" You will be given four numbers to choose from to answer the question. Similarly, you could also be asked, "The band room is 2,500 square feet, and the stage is 25% of the space in the auditorium. Describe the size of the band room compared to the stage." Possible answers could be "double," "triple," "smaller," or "equal." Not all questions will ask for an exact number but all have just one correct answer. Even if the answers do not specify an exact number, it is assumed that you will have used mathematical reasoning to figure out a correct answer. Questions that do not ask for exact numbers are not easier questions.

Answer choices are not designed to be tricky, but they won't be easy to choose correctly by guessing. Answer choices will not have one answer that is obviously incorrect. For example, if you are asked about the average cost of five items with prices all under $20.00, you won't find a choice such as "$422."

Answer choices will contain answers that might seem correct if you made a common mistake in reasoning or calculation. For example, if you are asked the median age of teachers at your school, that calls for a different mathematical calculation than if you were asked for the mode age. There may be an answer choice that correctly reflects the mode age of teachers, but this would not be the correct answer. Some answer choices also reflect common miscalculations, such as adding when a number should be multiplied. When choosing answers, make sure to

- Carefully read the question
- Check for any common or careless errors you may have made
- Recheck your thinking and your calculations

TALK TO YOURSELF!

Believe it or not, talking to yourself is a great WASL Mathematics strategy! You may not think about it, but you probably talk to yourself all the time when you are solving problems in everyday life, especially problems that have "steps." Much of mathematics calls for "linear thinking," meaning that problems are best solved when certain steps are followed in order.

Imagine that you are having a problem with your computer. You are typing an essay that is due the next day, when suddenly your mouse will not work. If you are a successful problem solver you will first identify the problem: "The mouse isn't working." You then go through a checklist of how to proceed. "Let me see if there is a program running that is messing up my word processing." You hit a few keys and don't see any interference. The next step is to look at the wireless mouse. You say to yourself, "Let me see if there is a problem with the mouse." You pick it up and it looks fine. Then you say, "Well, something on my desk could be the problem." And you are right! Your big metal stapler is blocking the signal between your mouse and the computer. You solved the problem, step by step, by talking to yourself.

The same strategy works for mathematical problems. Suppose you were asked, "Do you want to buy a used car? You'll need a 20% down payment on the car. The car costs $3,000.00. How many dollars will you have to save to make the down payment?" Identify the question asked, "This question has something to do with percentages." Then work through the processes involved, "I need to find a formula to help me find a part of a whole." Then say to yourself, "I will translate this into a sentence such as, 'Twenty-percent is what part of $3,000.00?'" From that point on, there are a number of ways to solve this problem, and you can choose whatever is easier for you. For example, you could convert 20% to its decimal form of .20 and then multiply by $3,000.00. You can then evaluate your answer by verbally reviewing your reasoning and checking your work. So, if your answer is $6,000.00, instead of the correct answer of $600.00, you should be able to find your error by repeating your calculations to yourself and asking yourself if the answer makes sense.

LEARN HOW TO "POWER GUESS"

Not everything you know was learned in a classroom. Part of what you know comes from just living your day-to-day life. When you take the Mathematics section of the WASL, you should use everything you have learned in school, but you should also use your experiences outside of the classroom to help you answer multiple-choice questions correctly. You might think to yourself, "Well, mathematics is different than other types of problems. There is just one correct answer. Things in mathematics are either right or wrong. If I don't know the answer right away, nothing else will help me get the question right." Although you might think that mathematics is different or harder, you still can use common sense thinking to help you do your best. Power guessing does not take the place of practice and knowledge, but it can help you to make reasonable choices by using what you know. Even if you eliminate one incorrect multiple-choice response, you have increased your chances of guessing correctly.

For example, take a look at this multiple-choice Mathematics question:

> Jeffrey's favorite music is "rock oldies," but his mother insists that the car radio be tuned to her favorite station, which plays "rock oldies" only about 12 minutes of every hour. What is the probability that Jeffrey's choice of music will be playing when his mom starts up the car?
>
> ○ **A.** $p = 0.12$
>
> ○ **B.** $p = 0.20$
>
> ○ **C.** $p = 0.90$
>
> ○ **D.** $p = 0.40$

Analysis: Suppose you forgot the formula to find probability. However, you know that probability can be simply described as "the chance that something will happen." The question tells you that Jeffrey's favorite music isn't played very often on his mother's chosen radio station. Now take a look at the answers. You will see that answer "C" shows a large number, 0.90, which suggests that Jeffrey would have a good chance of hearing his favorite tunes. That does not make logical sense. You know that 0.90 is probably incorrect, just using what you know about chance. (For example, if the news reported a 90% chance of rain, you wouldn't choose to schedule a softball practice). Thus, you eliminate choice "C". You are now left with three choices, and your chances of guessing the correct answer are improved. And now that you are thinking about the answer, the formula might come to mind. (The correct answer is "B," which is found by converting an hour to 60 minutes and then dividing, $12 \div 60 = 0.20$.)

ENHANCED MULTIPLE-CHOICE QUESTIONS

On the Mathematics WASL, you will always do your best if you thoroughly understand why you chose a certain multiple-choice answer. Some short-answer questions are labeled as "enhanced multiple-choice questions," and ask that you provide a short explanation of the reason that you chose that answer.

Enhanced multiple-choice questions are a lot like other short-answer questions. Your job is to briefly describe what you know about the answer you chose. For example, if you were asked to pick out the degrees of a missing angle on a triangle, where the two labeled angles were 32 and 48 degrees, you would choose the answer 100 degrees. For your enhanced response, you would write, "Because the total number of degrees in the angles of a triangle is always 180." Write simply, but use mathematical language. You're not communicating clearly and you won't get as much credit if you write, "Because there are just 100 degrees left in the triangle." You know what you mean, but your reasoning will not be clear when your test is scored, so be sure to show what you know when answering enhanced multiple-choice questions.

A SAMPLE ENHANCED MULTIPLE-CHOICE QUESTION

In a box of 48 chocolates, $\frac{2}{8}$ have nuts and 50% are cream-filled. How many chocolates in the box are caramel, if there are only 3 kinds of chocolates in the box?

● **A.** 12

○ **B.** 24

○ **C.** 8

○ **D.** 48

Construct a bar graph showing the number of each flavor of candy in the box.

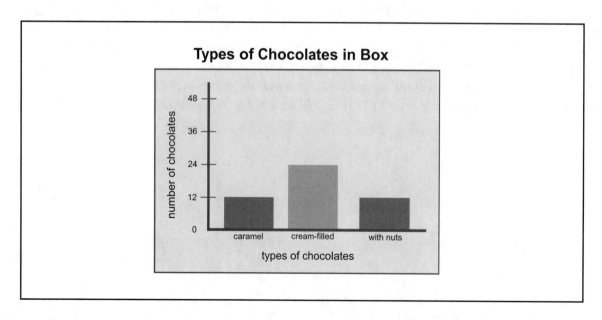

SHORT-ANSWER QUESTIONS

QUESTIONS CAN HELP YOU, SO READ THEM CAREFULLY

On both short-answer and extended-response items, the question should tell you what information to use in your answer. You might be told, "Use the information from the chart to find out how many more boxes of candy Amber had to sell in April to average selling 100 boxes a month." If you read the question carefully, you will know how to find the information to answer the question.

MAKE YOUR WRITING RIGHT

On the Mathematics WASL, you will be asked to give answers using words, numbers, graphs, figures, and drawings. These answers will be scored by people, not computers. You could be a math genius, but if your answer isn't legible, you won't receive credit for your knowledge.

One of the biggest problems many students have on tests is careless mistakes. Sometimes this carelessness comes from sloppy thinking, but a lot of the time these errors are caused by sloppy writing. Misaligning columns when adding or multiplying can result in incorrect answers. Writing numbers that can be mistaken for other numbers can cause miscalculations as well. For example, mistaking 23 for 28 is easy to do if your threes look like eights. You should have plenty of time to finish the WASL Mathematics questions, so take your time and write neatly. It will help you reduce careless errors and help the reader of your test to see all that you know.

WRITE WHAT YOU THINK AND HOW YOU THINK

Both short-answer and extended-response questions require you to show your work. To do your best, you must practice clearly communicating your answers; feeling comfortable using words, numbers, graphs, figures; and drawings; and knowing when to use them. You get credit for demonstrating how you arrived at your answer.

There is usually not one right way to think about a problem and find the right answer, and there usually isn't one correct way to show what you know. For example, suppose you were asked this short-answer question:

Brian is cutting pieces of triangular tile to make a designer bathroom for a customer. Each side of the tile is exactly six inches long. What is the angle of the top of the triangle?

Analysis: *First, you might want to draw a representation of a tile, like this:*

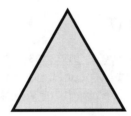

Then, you might write the following: All angles of this triangle are equal and so are the lengths of the sides of the triangle. All angles of a triangle always add up to 180 degrees, so each angle can be shown in the equation, 180 ÷ 3. Each angle would then equal 60 degrees.

Next, you might want to label each angle on the diagram.

You have successfully used numbers, words, and diagrams to clearly explain your reasoning and your correct answer.

GET FAMILIAR WITH THE TYPES OF SHORT-ANSWER QUESTIONS AND RESPONSES

Short-answer items can include more than words and numbers. You may be asked to read and interpret charts, diagrams, graphs, equations, and drawings.

Short-answer items ask students to show what they know using numbers, figures, diagrams, equations, or a few sentences. Some questions will instruct you as to what type of answer is needed, such as, "Draw a graph with *x*- and *y*-coordinates to illustrate this equation." Some questions let you figure out how best to respond. In preparation for the Mathematics WASL, you should practice expressing your answers using all of these possibilities.

The purpose of short-answer items is to measure your ability to

> • Show simple steps that lead to solving a mathematical problem.
> • Demonstrate your understanding of mathematical concepts.
> • Communicate a mathematical idea or result.
> • Use mathematical reasoning.

Thus, preparing for the Mathematics WASL is more than just learning to do "math problems." Instead, you want to train yourself to *think* about what you are doing, and why you are doing it. Then you will be better able show your reasoning and understanding of mathematics. Remember, the Mathematics WASL is much more than just a quiz. Instead, it is a measure of not just what you know, but how you use what you know to find correct answers.

LET'S TRY A SHORT-ANSWER EXAMPLE

Darcia's mother sees an advertisement on television about a new type of plant fertilizer called "Planter's Punch." This fertilizer will make tomatoes grow faster. Usually, tomatoes take three months of growth until they are ripe and ready to pick. However, this fertilizer causes the tomatoes to ripen 20% faster than usual. Darcia's mother uses this special fertilizer. Approximately how many days later can she expect to eat a ripe tomato?

There are several ways to solve this problem, but first you have to read the question carefully. The question asks for an "approximate" answer. That is good news because you won't need an exact answer. Ask yourself "why?" If you think about it, you will see that you are not expected to get an exact answer because each month can have a different number of days. Then, you will have to find a clear way of showing your work. You may want to first work out the calculations on the margins of your paper, and then show your work neatly. Or, if you feel confident, you can begin to show your work in the space provided.

Analysis: First, you have to show your answer in days. You know that on average there are about 30 days in a month. So you can now multiply the number of months by the number of days, 3 months x 30 days, and you will find that there are about 90 days in three months. If the tomatoes ripen 20% faster, you then need find 20% of 90 days: 90 days x .20 = 18. Subtract 90 – 18 = 72 days, finding that the tomatoes will be ripe in about 72 days.

Your answer should show your mathematical thinking and be easy to read. It might look like this:

It will take about __72__ days to have a ripe tomato.

1 month = 30 days; 30 days x 3 months = 90 days.

20% of 90 days = 18 days (90 x .20 = 18)

90 days - 18 days = 72 days.

EXTENDED-RESPONSE ITEMS

TO DO YOUR BEST ON EXTENDED-RESPONSE ITEMS, PRACTICE SHORT-ANSWER ITEMS FIRST

Like short-answer questions, extended-response questions require thinking and ask you to respond in a variety of possible ways. Many students find it more effective to first feel comfortable with short-answer questions, and then move on to tackling extended-response questions.

USE YOUR PENCIL TO YOUR ADVANTAGE!

Don't hesitate to make an outline of your answer on the margins of your test booklet. Look at extended-response items as you would an essay question and take some time to write down the structure of your response. Then, add details. Thinking first and writing later is always a good idea.

BE THE TEACHER FOR THE DAY!

Extended-response answers require YOU to be the teacher! Extended responses often ask that you explain your answer in a way that is complete and understandable. Ask yourself, "If I were explaining my answer to a friend, would he or she understand?" Express your answers in a step-by-step manner, explaining your reasoning as you proceed. Don't assume that your "student" knows everything or can read your mind.

DON'T AVOID EXTENDED-RESPONSE ITEMS

Extended-response items can be intimidating for some students, especially if they feel that they are weaker in mathematics than in other subjects. While there are fewer extended-response items on the WASL, your answers are important in helping you do well on the mathematics test.

Keep in mind that even a partially correct answer will increase your score, and there is no penalty for trying. If you find yourself feeling anxious about these more complex questions, review the section of this book about Test Anxiety, or talk to your math teacher or school counselor.

EXTENDED-RESPONSE QUESTIONS AREN'T ALWAYS "HARDER" QUESTIONS

Extended-response questions basically ask how you arrived at your answer. The actual mathematics may not be complicated or advanced. Remember, the purpose of learning mathematics is to help you solve problems in school and in the rest of your life. Some mathematics will come without much thinking, such as knowing that 10 x 10 equals 100. However, when you have to figure out a problem in college, or at the hardware store, you will need to put on your "thinking cap" to solve the problem. So, don't shy away from extended-response items because you tell yourself, "This has to be WAY too hard." As you read the question, start to think about how you would describe your thinking and your answer, and don't forget to use mathematical vocabulary in your response.

A SAMPLE EXTENDED-RESPONSE QUESTION

Ms. Chang owns an office building. She needs to buy 10,000 square feet of carpet to improve the hallways and offices. Ms. Chang is told that there are several types of carpet that she can purchase. Each type of carpet has a different cost, but each type also has different strengths; some carpets last longer than others before they need to be replaced. Ms. Chang wants the building to look good for the next ten years. Here is the information she was given by the carpet saleswoman:

Type of Carpet	Cost per sq ft	Years Until Replacement
Grade C carpet	$2.00	3 Years
Grade B carpet	$3.00	4 Years
Grade A carpet	$7.00	15 Years

Which carpet should Ms. Chang choose?

Explain in detail your answer using words, numbers, and/or diagrams.

Where do you begin? First, talk to yourself! Read the question slowly and read the chart as well. You know that you have to cover 10,000 square feet, and that the carpet needs to last for 10 years. So, you have to figure out if it is better to get the most expensive carpet, or carpet that is less expensive but doesn't last as long. (See, the question takes some thinking, but it isn't using fancy mathematics!)

Analysis: The first thing to do is to calculate the initial cost of carpet:

Grade C carpet $2 x 10,000 sq. ft. = $20,000

Grade B carpet $3 x 10,000 sq. ft. = $30,000

Grade A carpet $7 x 10,000 sq. ft. = $70,000

Now, you have to figure the cost of the carpet over 10 years.

Grade C carpet lasts 3 years. How often will it have to be replaced over 10 years? Simply divide 10 by 3, and you will find the answer to be 3.3. Or, you could create a simple visual timeline drawing to illustrate the same idea. Either way, don't be fooled by the decimal! Over 10 years, Grade C carpet will have to be replaced 4 times (years one through three, years four through six, years seven through nine, and then AGAIN beginning in year 10). The carpet might start out as inexpensive, but the total cost over 10 years would be $20,000 x 4 = $80,000.

Grade B carpet lasts 4 years. Either dividing or looking at your timeline, you see that it will have to be replaced three times over 10 years. Thus, the total cost is $30,000 x 3 = $90,000.

Grade A carpet costs $70,000 but it lasts 15 years. Ms. Chang will only have to purchase carpet one time in ten years. The total cost over 10 years will be $70,000 if she purchases Grade A carpet.

After showing your calculations, you can display your data by using diagrams like the bar graph and timeline shown below. Remember to use mathematical language and write legibly.

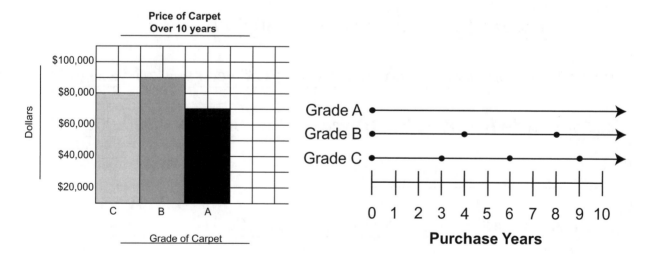

Your answer should show your mathematical thinking and be easy to read. It might look like this:

Ms. Chang should choose _Grade A_ carpet.

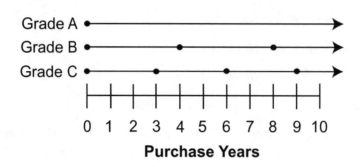

Grade C carpet: $2 x 10,000 sq. ft. = $20,000

Grade C carpet lasts 3 years. 10 years ÷ 3 years = 3.3 years.

Cost of Grade C carpet for 10 years; 4 x $20,000 = $80,000.

Grade B carpet: $3 x 10,000 sq. ft. = $30,000

Grade B carpet lasts 4 years. 10 years ÷ 4 years = 2.5 years.

Cost of Grade B carpet for 10 years; 3 x $30,000 = $90,000.

Grade A carpet: $7 x 10,000 sq. ft. = $70,000

Grade A carpet lasts 15 years.

Cost of Grade A carpet for 10 years = $70,000.

MATHEMATICS

INTRODUCTION

The Mathematics Assessment of the Washington Assessment of Student Learning (WASL) measures your understanding of the mathematical skills you have been taught in school through tenth grade. Within this section of the WASL, you will find a variety of question formats, including multiple choice, short answer, enhanced multiple choice (scored as short-answer questions), and extended response. These different question formats give you the opportunity to demonstrate your knowledge in many different ways, through numbers, words, pictures, graphs, and charts.

This *Show What You Know® on the WASL Mathematics for Grade 10, Student Self-Study Workbook* contains the following:

- The Essential Academic Learning Requirements (EALRs), Components, Grade Level Expectations (GLEs), Item Distribution, and Scoring Guides for the Grade 10 Washington Assessment of Student Learning in Mathematics.

- The Mathematics Practice Tutorial contains a sample question for each EALR tested, sample responses, and an answer key with in-depth analysis.

- Two full-length Mathematics Assessments with sample responses, correlation charts, and answer keys with in-depth analysis.

Show What You Know® on the WASL Mathematics for Grade 10, Student Self-Sudy Workbook will help you practice your test-taking skills. The Mathematics Practice Tutorial and the two full-length Mathematics Assessments (Mathematics Assessment One—Session One and Session Two, Mathematics Assessment Two—Session One and Session Two) have been created to model the Grade 10 Washington Assessment of Student Learning in Mathematics.

UNDERSTANDING GRADE LEVEL EXPECTATIONS

An **Essential Academic Learning Requirement** (EALR) is a broad statement of the learning that applies to grades K–10.

EALR 1: The student understands and applies the concepts and procedures of mathematics.

The **Component** is a K–10 statement that further defines the EALR. There is at least one Component for each EALR.

Component 1.1 Understand and apply concepts and procedures from number sense.

The **Grade Level Expectation** (GLE) is a statement of cognitive demand, using the essential content or process to be learned. The statement, specific to one or more grades, defines the component.

GLE 1.1.1 Understand and apply scientific notation. **W**

- Read and use scientific and exponential notation. [MC, RL]

- Identify a real-life situation to match a particular number written in scientific or exponential notation and justify the answer. [MC, RL]

The **Evidence of Learning** is a bulleted list of student demonstrations that provide educators with common illustration of the learning.

- Use scientific or exponential notation to simplify a problem. [RL, MC]

- Illustrate the meaning of scientific notation using pictures, diagrams, or numbers. [CU]

- Read and translate numbers represented in scientific notation from calculators and other technology, tables, and charts.

The GLE **Numbering System** identifies the EALR, the Component, and the GLE. For example, in the number 1.1.1 the first number stands for the EALR, the second number for the Component, the third for the GLE. Note: Grade levels or bands are not referenced in the numbering system. Grade Level Expectations with a **W** denote the specific Expectations which are eligible for the WASL. Not all GLEs have a **W**. Note: Narrowing instruction to just those expectations with a **W** may adversely affect student success.

ESSENTIAL ACADEMIC LEARNING REQUIREMENTS FOR MATHEMATICS

EALR 1: The student understands and applies the concepts and procedures of mathematics.

Component 1.1: Understand and apply concepts and procedures from number sense.

Number and numeration

W   **GLE 1.1.1 Demonstrate understanding of the concept and symbolic representation of numbers written in scientific notation.**
- Read and use scientific and exponential notation. [MC, RL]
- Identify a real-life situation to match a particular number written in scientific or exponential notation and justify the answer. [MC, RL]
- Use scientific or exponential notation to simplify a problem. [RL, MC]
- Illustrate the meaning of scientific notation using pictures, diagrams, or numbers. [CU]
- Read and translate numbers represented in scientific notation from calculators and other technology, tables, and charts.

W   **GLE 1.1.4 Demonstrate understanding of and apply the concepts of both direct and inverse proportion.**
- Explain a method for determining whether a real-world problem involves direct proportion or inverse proportion. [SP, CU, MC]
- Explain a method for solving a real-world problem involving direct proportion. [CU, MC]
- Explain a method for solving a real-world problem involving inverse proportion. [CU, MC]
- Solve problems using direct or inverse models (e.g., similarity, age of car *vs.* worth). [SP, MC]
- Explain, illustrate, or describe examples of direct proportion. [CU]
- Explain, illustrate, or describe examples of inverse proportion. [CU]
- Use direct or inverse proportion to determine a number of objects or a measurement in a given situation.

Computation

W   **GLE 1.1.6 Complete multi-step computations with combinations of rational numbers, including whole number powers and square roots of perfect squares, using order of operations.**
- Complete multi-step computations using order of operations in situations involving combinations of rational numbers including whole number exponents and square roots of square numbers. [MC]
- Calculate using order of operations on all forms of rational numbers (e.g., $(3 \cdot 2 + 5) 2 - 8$, $22 + 32$).
- Use properties to reorder and rearrange expressions to compute more efficiently. [RL]

Key	
SP: Solves Problems	**RL:** Reasons Logically
CU: Communicates Understanding	**MC:** Makes Connections

Estimation

W   **GLE 1.1.8 Use estimation to determine the reasonableness of answers in situations involving multi-step computations with rational numbers, including whole number powers and square roots.**

- Identify when an approximation is appropriate. [MC]
- Explain situations involving rational numbers where estimates are sufficient and others for which exact value is required. [CU]
- Justify why an estimate would be used rather than an exact answer in a given situation. [CU]
- Describe various strategies used during estimation involving integers. [CU]
- Use estimation to predict or to verify the reasonableness of calculated results. [RL]

Component 1.2: Understand and apply concepts and procedures from measurement.

Attributes, units, and systems

W   **GLE 1.2.1 Demonstrate understanding of how a change in one linear dimension affects surface area and volume or how changes in two linear dimensions affect perimeter, area, and volume.**

- Describe and compare the impact that a change in one or more dimensions has on objects (e.g., how doubling one dimension of a cube affects the surface area and volume). [CU, MC]
- Describe how changes in the dimensions of objects affect perimeter, area, and volume in real world situations (e.g., how does the change in the diameter of an oil drum affect the area and volume). [CU, MC]
- Solve problems by deriving the changes in two dimensions necessary to obtain a desired surface area and/or volume (e.g., given a box with certain dimensions, make the volume of the box y cubic units by changing two dimensions of the box). [SP]
- Compare a given change in one or two dimensions on the perimeter, area, surface area, or volumes of two objects.
- Determine the change in one dimension given a change in perimeter, area, volume, or surface area.

W   **GLE 1.2.3 Demonstrate understanding of how to convert within the US or the metric system to achieve an appropriate level of precision.**

- Convert within a system to a unit size appropriate to a given situation.
- Convert to a larger unit within a system while maintaining the same level of precision (e.g., represent 532 centimeters to 5.32 meters).
- Convert to a smaller unit within a system to increase the precision of a derived unit of measurement.

Key

SP: Solves Problems	**RL:** Reasons Logically
CU: Communicates Understanding	**MC:** Makes Connections

Procedures and estimation

W   **GLE 1.2.5 Use formulas to determine measurements of prisms or cylinders.**
- Explain how to use a formula for finding the volume of a prism or cylinder. [CU, MC]
- Use a formula to find the volume of a prism or cylinder. [RL, MC]
- Use a formula to derive a dimension of a right prism or right cylinder given other measures.
- Use formulas to describe and compare the surface areas and volumes of two or more right prisms and/or right cylinders. [RL]
- Use formulas to obtain measurements needed to describe a right cylinder or a right prism.

W   **GLE 1.2.6 Identify situations in which estimated measurements are sufficient; use estimation to obtain reasonable measurements at an appropriate level of precision.**
- Estimate quantities using derived units of measure (e.g., distance or time using miles per hour, cost using unit cost). [MC]
- Estimate derived units of measure (e.g., miles per hour, people/year, grams/cubic centimeters). [MC]
- Apply a process that can be used to find a reasonable estimate for the volume of prisms, pyramids, cylinders, and cones.
- Estimate volume and surface area for right cylinders and right prisms.

Component 1.3: Understand and apply concepts and procedures from geometric sense.

Properties and relationships

W   **GLE 1.3.1 Demonstrate understanding of the relationships among 1-dimensional, 2-dimensional and 3-dimensional shapes and figures.**
- Identify and label one- and two-dimensional characteristics (rays, lines, end points, line segments, vertices, and angles) in three-dimensional figures. [CU]
- Match or draw three-dimensional objects from different perspectives using the same properties and relationships (e.g., match to the correct net, draw the top view). [RL]
- Draw and label with names and symbols nets of right prisms and right cylinders. [RL, CU]
- Describe everyday objects in terms of their geometric characteristics. [CU]
- Describe or classify various shapes based on their characteristics.
- Make and test conjectures about two-dimensional and three-dimensional shapes and their individual attributes and relationships using physical, symbolic, and technological models (e.g., diagonal of a rectangle or prism is the longest interior segment; what figures make up cross-sections of a given three-dimensional shape). [SP, RL, CU, MC]

Key	
SP: Solves Problems	**RL:** Reasons Logically
CU: Communicates Understanding	**MC:** Makes Connections

Properties and relationships

W   **GLE 1.3.2 Draw, describe, and/or compare 1-dimensional, 2-dimensional and 3-dimensional shapes and figures, including prisms, cylinders, cones, and pyramids.**

- Construct geometric figures using a variety of tools and technologies (e.g., angle bisectors, perpendicular bisectors, triangles given specific characteristics). [MC]
- Draw a plane shape and justify the answer given a set of characteristics. [RL, CU]
- Use the properties of two-dimensional and three-dimensional shapes to solve mathematical problems (e.g., find the width of a river based on similar triangles; given a set of parallel lines, a transversal, and an angle, find the other angles). [SP, RL, CU, MC]
- Compare two-dimensional and three-dimensional shapes according to characteristics including faces, edges, and vertices, using actual and virtual modeling. [RL, CU]
- Use technology to generate two- and three-dimensional models of geometric figures with given geometric characteristics (e.g., generate a two-dimensional animation using pentagons with fixed coordinates for one edge). [RL, SP]
- Create a three-dimensional scale drawing with particular geometric characteristics. [SP, CU, MC]

Locations and transformations

W   **GLE 1.3.3 Use geometric properties to describe or identify the location of points on coordinate grids.**

- Use coordinates to describe or identify the location of objects on coordinate grids.
- Describe geometric characteristics of two-dimensional objects using coordinates on a grid. [MC]
- Describe the location of points that satisfy given conditions (e.g., the set of points equidistant from a given point; a point equidistant from a given set of points). [CU]
- Represent situations on a coordinate grid or describe the location of points that satisfy given conditions (e.g., locate a gas station to be equidistant from given cities; locate a staking point to maximize the grazing area of a tethered goat). [MC, SP, RL]
- Use tools and technology to draw objects on a coordinate grid based on given conditions. [CU]
- Identify, interpret, and use the meaning of slope of a line as a rate of change using physical, symbolic, and technological models. [SP, RL, MC]

Key	
SP: Solves Problems	**RL:** Reasons Logically
CU: Communicates Understanding	**MC:** Makes Connections

Locations and transformations

W **GLE 1.3.4 Use multiple transformations, including translations, reflections, and/or rotations, to create congruent figures in any or all of the four quadrants.**

- Apply multiple transformations to create congruent and similar figures in any or all of the four quadrants.
- Use multiple transformations (combinations of translations, reflections, or rotations) to draw an image. [RL]
- Use dilation (expansion or contraction) of a given shape to form a similar shape. [RL, CU]
- Determine the final coordinates of a point after a series of transformations. [RL, CU]
- Examine figures to determine rotational symmetry about the center of the shape. [RL, MC]
- Define a set of transformations that would map one onto the other given two similar shapes. [SP, RL]
- Create a design with or without technology using a combination of two or more transformations with one or two two-dimensional figures. [SP, RL]
- Use technology to create two- and three-dimensional animations using combinations of transformations. [MC, SP, RL]

Component 1.4: Understand and apply concepts and procedures from probability and statistics.

Probability

W **GLE 1.4.1 Demonstrate understanding of the concepts of dependent and independent events.**
- Compare the probabilities of dependent and independent events. [CU, MC]
- Determine and justify whether the outcome of a first event affects the probability of a later event (e.g., drawing cards from a deck with or without replacement). [CU]
- Explain the difference between dependent and independent events. [CU]
- Explain and give examples of compound events. [CU]

W **GLE 1.4.2 Determine and use probabilities of dependent and independent events.**
- Generate the outcomes and probability of multiple independent and dependent events using a model or procedure (e.g., tree diagram, area model, counting procedures).
- Generate the outcomes and probability of events using a counting procedure (e.g., the number of license plates that can be made with three letters and three numbers; winning the lottery). [MC]
- Explain the relationship between theoretical probability and empirical frequency of dependent events using simulations with and without technology. [CU]
- Create a simple game based on independent probabilities wherein all players have an equal probability of winning. [MC, SP]
- Create a simple game based on compound probabilities. [MC, SP]
- Determine the sample space for independent or dependent events.

Key	
SP: Solves Problems	**RL:** Reasons Logically
CU: Communicates Understanding	**MC:** Makes Connections

Statistics

W **GLE 1.4.3 Identify possible sources of bias in questions, data collection methods, samples, and/or measures of central tendency for a situation and describe how such bias can be controlled.**
- Evaluate methods and technology used to investigate a research question. [CU, MC]
- Collect data using appropriate methods.
- Use technology appropriately to collect data. [RL, MC]
- Identify appropriate data collection methods that might impact the accuracy of the results of a given situation. [RL, CU]
- Determine whether the sample for a given study was from a representative sample.
- Determine whether the methods of data collection used were appropriate for a given question or population. [RL]

W **GLE 1.4.5 Draw a reasonable line to describe the data represented by a scatter plot and determine whether a straight line is an appropriate way to describe the trend in the data.**
- Determine whether the underlying model for a set of data is linear. [RL, MC]
- Decide and explain whether it is appropriate to extend a given data set following a line of best fit. [RL, MC]
- Determine whether a linear prediction from a given set of data is appropriate for the data and support the decision with data. [MC].
- Determine whether an equation for a line is appropriate for a given set of data and support the judgment with data. [RL, MC]
- Use technology to generate data to fit a linear model. [SP, MC]

W **GLE 1.4.6 Use statistics to support different points of view and/or evaluate a statistical argument based on data.**
- Identify trends in a set of data in order to make a prediction based on the information. [CU, MC]
- Justify a prediction or an inference based on a set of data. [CU, MC]
- State possible factors that may influence a trend but not be reflected in the data (e.g., population growth of deer vs. availability of natural resources or hunting permits). [MC, CU, RL]
- Analyze a set of statistics to develop a logical point of view. [RL. CU, MC]
- Justify or refute claims and supporting arguments based on data. [CU, MC]
- Determine whether statistics have been used or misused to support a point of view or argument and support the evaluation with data. [RL]

Key	
SP: Solves Problems	**RL:** Reasons Logically
CU: Communicates Understanding	**MC:** Makes Connections

Component 1.5: Understand and apply concepts and procedures from algebraic sense.

Patterns and Functions

W   **GLE 1.5.1 Recognize, extend or create a pattern or sequence of pairs of numbers representing a linear function.**
- Identify, extend, or create a geometric or arithmetic sequence or pattern. [RL, CU]
- Translate among equivalent numerical, graphical, and algebraic forms of a linear function. [RL, MC]
- Make predictions based on a pattern or sequence.

W   **GLE 1.5.2 Identify or write a rule to describe a pattern, sequence, and/or linear function.**
- Find the equation of a line in a variety of ways (e.g., from a table, graph, slope-intercept, point-slope, two points). [RL, MC]
- Generate and use rules for a pattern to make predictions about future events (e.g., population growth, future sales, growth of corn stalks, future value of savings account). [SP, RL, MC]
- Identify or write an equation or rule to describe a pattern, sequence, and/or a linear function. [RL, CU, MC]
- Write an equation for a line given a set of information (e.g., two points, point-slope, etc.). [CU, MC]
- Write a recursive definition of a geometric pattern (e.g., Start and New = Old * Number). [CU, MC]
- Represent systems of equations and inequalities graphically. [RL, MC]
- Write a story that represents a given linear equation or expression. [CU, MC]
- Write an expression, equation, or inequality with two variables representing a linear model of a real-world problem. [CU, MC]

Symbols and Notations

W   **GLE 1.5.4 Use variables to write expressions, linear equations, and inequalities that represent situations involving whole number powers and square and cube roots.**
- Identify and use variable quantities to read and write expressions and equations to represent situations that can be described using repeated addition (e.g., models that are linear in nature). [CU, MC]
- Identify and use variable quantities to read and write expressions and equations to represent situations that can be described using repeated multiplication (e.g., models that are exponential such as savings accounts and early stages of population growth). [CU, MC]
- Recognize and write equations in recursive form for additive models (e.g., starting value, New = Old + some number). [CU, MC]
- Recognize and write equations in recursive form for multiplicative models (e.g., starting value, New = Old **x** some number). [CU, MC]
- Select an expression or equation to represent a given real world situation. [MC]

Key	
SP: Solves Problems	**RL:** Reasons Logically
CU: Communicates Understanding	**MC:** Makes Connections

Evaluating and solving

W **GLE 1.5.5 Simplify expressions.**
- Simplify expressions and evaluate formulas involving exponents.
- Justify a simplification of an expression involving exponents. [RL, CU]
- Use multiple mathematical strategies and properties to simplify expressions.

W **GLE 1.5.6 Solve multi-step equations and systems of equations.**
- Rearrange formulas to solve for a particular variable (e.g., given , solve for *h*). [MC, CU]
- Solve real-world situations involving linear relationships and verify that the solution makes sense in relation to the problem. [SP, RL, CU, MC]
- Find the solution to a system of linear equations using tables, graphs, and symbols. [CU, MC]
- Interpret solutions of systems of equations. [CU, MC]
- Use systems of equations to analyze and solve real-life problems. [SP, CU, MC]
- Determine when two linear options yield the same outcome (e.g., given two different investment or profit options, determine when both options will yield the same result).
- Use systems of equations to determine the most advantageous outcome given a situation (e.g., given two investment options, determine under what conditions each will yield the best result.). [MC, SP]

Key	
SP: Solves Problems	**RL:** Reasons Logically
CU: Communicates Understanding	**MC:** Makes Connections

EALR 2: The student uses mathematics to define and solve problems.

Component 2.1: Define Problems.

Example: The following are the times (in seconds) of the Olympics in the given years. Using this information, is it reasonable to believe that the women will run as fast as the men in this event? Justify your answer using this data:

Year	Men's	Women's	Year	Men's	Women's
1948	10.3	11.9	1976	10.06	11.08
1952	10.4	11.5	1980	10.25	11.06
1956	10.5	11.5	1984	9.99	10.97
1960	10.2	11.0	1988	9.92	10.54
1964	10	11.4	1992	9.96	10.82
1968	9.95	11.0	1996	9.84	10.94
1972	10.14	11.07	2000	9.87	10.75

W   **GLE 2.1.1 Identify questions to be answered in complex situations.**

- Use strategies to become informed about the situation (e.g., listing information; examine the table for patterns; create a scatter plot to look for patterns; asking questions).
- Summarize the problem (e.g., there are Olympic winning times over the past 50 years; both men's and women's times are decreasing; will there come a time when women run faster than men).
- Define the problem (e.g., if the pattern continues in the same fashion, will women run faster than men and, if so, when will that occur).

W   **GLE 2.1.2 Recognize when information is missing or extraneous.**

- Determine whether enough information is given to find a solution (e.g., list what is needed to be found; extend the pattern to see if women's times will be less).
- Identify or clarify the question the problem presents.

W   **GLE 2.1.3 Identify what is known and unknown in complex situations.**

- Formulate or identify additional question(s) that need to be answered in order to find a solution to a given problem.
- Identify the "known" and "unknown" information in a given problem situation.

Component 2.2: Construct Solutions.

[W] GLE 2.2.1 Select and organize relevant information.

• Organize relevant information from multiple sources (e.g., create a list of known and unknown information; create a scatter plot of men's and women's times vs. time on the same coordinate axis to analyze the patterns).

[W] GLE 2.2.2 Use appropriate concepts and procedures from number sense, measurement, geometric sense, probability and statistics, and algebraic sense.

• Select and apply appropriate mathematical tools to devise a strategy in a situation (e.g., if the data, in either tabular or graphical form, suggest a linear relationship, plan to find a linear equation for each set of data; solve those equations simultaneously [or use technology to find the intersection of the two lines] to answer the question). If the data pattern suggests a non-linear model, plan to project what the pattern is and extend that pattern.

• Implement the plan devised to solve the problem (e.g., solve the set of simultaneous equations to arrive at a time where the two times are the same).

• Use mathematics to solve the problem (e.g., use algebra to write equations for the two linear models, solve the system of equations using either symbols or technology).

[W] GLE 2.2.3. Use a variety of strategies and approaches.

• Identify when an approach is unproductive and modify or try a new approach (e.g., if the result does not make sense in the context, return to the plan to see if something has gone wrong and adjust accordingly).

[W] GLE 2.2.4. Determine whether a solution is viable, mathematically correct, and answers the question(s) asked.

• Check the solution to see if it works (e.g., the solution may be a partial year [i.e., 2003.6]; decide how to deal with this and also if the year is reasonable [i.e., 1925 does not make sense given the context]).

EALR 3: The student uses mathematical reasoning.

Component 3.1: Analyze information.

W **GLE 3.1.1. Interpret, compare, and integrate mathematical information from multiple sources.**

- Use the properties of two-dimensional and three-dimensional figures to solve mathematical problems (e.g., find the width of a river based on similar triangles; given a set of parallel lines, a transversal, and an angle, find the other angles).
- Interpret mathematical information or results.
- Compare mathematical information in text, graphs, tables, diagrams, and/or pictorial representations.
- Compare information in order to answer a question.
- Identify the agreement (or differences) between information, diagrams, and/or pictorial representations.
- Compare patterns or trends shown by data or other information.
- Integrate information from two or more sources to develop an interpretation.

Component 3.2: Conclude.

W **GLE 3.2.1 Draw conclusions and support them using inductive and deductive reasoning.**

- Make and test conjectures about two-dimensional and three-dimensional figures and their individual attributes and relationships using physical, symbolic, and technological models (e.g., diagonal of a rectangle or prism is the longest interior segment; what figures make up cross-sections of a given three-dimensional shape). (1.3.1)

W **GLE 3.2.2 Evaluate procedures and make needed revisions.**

- Compare and describe the volume of cylinders, cones, and prisms when an attribute is changed (e.g., the area of the base, the height of solid). (1.2.4)
- Draw a plane shape of a given set of characteristics and justify the answer. (1.3.2)
- Identify trends in a set of data in order to make a prediction based on the information. (1.4.6)
- Use statistics to support different points of view. (1.4.6)
- Examine claims and supporting arguments based on data and make needed revisions. (1.4.6)
- Evaluate procedures used and/or the results based on a given partial or complete solution to a problem.

Component 3.3: Verify results.

W **GLE 3.3.1 Justify results using inductive and deductive reasoning.**
- Compare and contrast similar two-dimensional figures and shapes using properties of two-dimensional figures and shapes. (1.3.2)
- Find a reasonable estimate for the volume of prisms, pyramids, cylinders, and cones. (1.2.6)

W **GLE 3.3.2 Check for reasonableness of results.**
- Items may ask students to use various concepts, procedures, and problem-solving strategies to construct a solution for a given situation and then to check for reasonableness of results.

W **GLE 3.3.3 Validate thinking and mathematical ideas using models, known facts, patterns, relationships, counter examples, and/or proportional reasoning.**
- Examine a set of data, research other sources to see if the data is consistent, find articles written to see if the data makes sense, to develop a logical point of view and to support that view. (1.4.6)

EALR 4: The student communicates knowledge and understanding in both everyday and mathematical language.

Component 4.1: Gather information.

W **GLE 4.1.1 Develop or select and follow an efficient system for collecting mathematical information for a given purpose.**
- Collect data efficiently on the outcomes of first events and later events to determine and justify how the first event affects the probability of later events (e.g., drawing cards from a deck with or without replacement). (1.4.1)
- List or describe the general procedure/order of steps of a plan to gather exactly the information sought and no irrelevant information.

W **GLE 4.1.2 Extract mathematical information for a given purpose from multiple, self-selected sources using reading, listening, and/or observation.**
- State possible factors that may influence a trend but not be reflected in the data (e.g., population growth of deer vs. availability of natural resources or hunting permits). (1.4.6)
- Extract and explain or describe mathematical information from various sources such as pictures, symbols, text, tables, charts, graphs, diagrams, and models.
- Write questions that could be answered using data sources such as magazines, newspapers, menus, sales and travel brochures, TV and bus schedules, or sales receipts.

Component 4.2: Organize, represent, and share information.

W   **GLE 4.2.1 Organize, clarify, and refine mathematical information relevant to a given purpose.**

• Develop an argument to support a given point of view and set of statistics. (1.4.6)

• Explain or represent mathematical information using pictures, tables, graphs, 2- or 3-dimensional drawings, or other appropriate forms including titles and labels, appropriate and consistent scale(s), and accurate data display for a given audience and/or purpose.

W   **GLE 4.2.2 Use everyday and mathematical language and notation in appropriate and efficient forms to clearly express or represent complex ideas and information.**

• Explain how division of measurements produces a derived unit of measurement (e.g., miles traveled divided by hours traveled yields the derived unit [miles per hour]). (1.2.2)

• Describe the location of points that satisfy given conditions (e.g., the set of points equidistant from a given point; a point equidistant from a given set of points). (1.3.3)

• Describe and compare the impact that a change in one or more dimensions has on objects (e.g., doubling the edge of a cube affects the surface area). (1.2.1)

• Explain the relationship between theoretical probability and empirical frequency of dependent events using simulations with and without technology. (1.4.2)

W   **GLE 4.2.3 Explain and/or represent complex mathematical ideas and information in ways appropriate for audience and purpose in a context that is relevant to tenth grade students.**

• Clearly explain or represent mathematical information using pictures, tables, graphs, 2- or 3-dimensional drawings, or other appropriate forms including titles and labels, appropriate and consistent scale(s), and accurate data display for a given audience and/or purpose.

• Clearly explain or describe mathematical ideas, facts, properties, procedures, or strategies in a way that is appropriate for a given audience and/or purpose using mathematical language and notation.

EALR 5: The student understands how mathematical ideas connect within mathematics, to other subject areas, and to real-life situations.

Component 5.1: Relate concepts and procedures within mathematics.

W **GLE 5.1.1 Use concepts and procedures from two or more of the mathematics content strands in a given problem or situation.**

- Identify which of four mathematical models or representations is equivalent to the given mathematical model or representation.
- Estimate derived units of measure (e.g., miles per hour, people/year, grams/cubic centimeters). (1.2.6)
- Determine the final coordinates of a point after a series of transformations. (1.3.4)

W **GLE 5.1.2 Relate and use different mathematical models and representations of the same situations.**

- Identify, interpret, and use the meaning of slope of a line as a rate of change using concrete, symbolic, and technological models. (1.2.2)
- Construct one-dimensional, two-dimensional, and three-dimensional geometric figures using a variety of tools and technologies (e.g., angle bisectors, perpendicular bisectors, triangles given specific characteristics). (1.3.2)
- Find the equation of a line in a variety of ways (e.g., from a table, graph, slope-intercept, point-slope, two points). (1.5.1)
- Find the solution to a system of linear equations using tables, graphs and symbols. (1.5.6)

ABOUT THE MATHEMATICS WASL

The Grade 10 Mathematics Assessment will test Content (number sense, measurement, geometric sense, probability and statistics, and algebraic sense) as well as Process (solves problems and reasons logically, communicates understanding, and makes connections). The Mathematics Assessment is given in two sessions, Session One and Session Two.

For the Mathematics Assessment there are four different types of questions: multiple choice, enhanced multiple choice, short answer, and extended response. For Session One, you will be allowed to use calculators, rulers, protractors, and manipulatives. Dictionaries, thesauruses, and scratch paper are not allowed on either session of the Mathematics test.

ITEM DISTRIBUTION ON THE WASL FOR GRADE 10 MATHEMATICS

Essential Academic Learning Requirement	Strand	Multiple-Choice Items	Short-Answer Items**	Extended-Response Items	Total Number of Points
Concepts & Procedures of Mathematics (CP)	Number Sense (5)*	3 – 5	1 – 2	0	6 – 7
	Measurement (4)*	3 – 5	1 – 2	0	6 – 7
	Geometric Sense (2)*	3 – 5	1 – 2	0	6 – 7
	Probability and Statistics (3)*	3 – 5	1 – 2	0	6 – 7
	Algebraic Sense (3)*	3 – 5	1 – 2	0	6 – 7
Solves Problems (SP) & Reasons Logically (RL) (5)*		0 – 2	2 – 3	2 – 3	12 – 18
Communicates Understanding (CU) (2)*		0	1 – 2	1 – 2	8 – 10
Makes Connections (MC) (1)*		2 – 4	1 – 2	0	6 – 7
Total Number of Items		**27**	**11**	**4**	**42**
Total Number of Points		**27**	**22**	**16**	**65**

Numbers in parentheses represent the number of Learning Targets in each Strand as assessed in the Washington Assessment of Student Learning.

** Includes enhanced multiple-choice questions. No more than three items will be enhanced multiple-choice questions.

SCORING

On the WASL for Grade 10 Mathematics Assessment, each multiple-choice item is worth one point. Short-answer items and enhanced multiple-choice items will be scored on a scale of zero to two points, and extended-response items will be scored on a scale of zero to four points. The scoring criteria will focus on the understanding of mathematical ideas, information, and solutions, and will disregard conventions of writing (complete sentences, usage/grammar, spelling, capitalization, punctuation, and paragraphing), as long as the wording of the response does not interfere with the mathematical communication.

TYPICAL DISTRIBUTION OF SCORE POINTS BY ITEM TYPE

Type	Number of Items	Total Possible Points	Percent of Total Score
Multiple Choice	27	27	42%
Short Answer (including Enhanced Multiple Choice)	11	22	58%
Extended Response	4	16	
Total	42	65	100%

SCORING RULES FOR SHORT-ANSWER ITEMS AND ENHANCED MULTIPLE-CHOICE ITEMS

SCORING RUBRIC FOR SHORT-ANSWER ITEMS THAT ASSESS <u>CONCEPTS AND PROCEDURES</u> (CONTENT STRANDS):

A **2-point** response shows understanding of the concept or procedure, appropriate use of applicable information and procedures, and accurate results.

A **1-point** response shows partial understanding of the concept or procedure with errors in the use of applicable information, procedures, or computations that limit the viability of an answer.

A **0-point** response shows very little or no understanding of the concept or procedure.

SCORING RUBRIC FOR SHORT-ANSWER ITEMS THAT ASSESS <u>SOLVES PROBLEMS</u> (SR01):

A **2-point** response defines a problem by identifying questions to be answered, missing or extraneous information, and/or what is known or unknown in a given situation.

A **1-point** response partially defines a problem by identifying some questions to be answered, some missing or extraneous information, or some of what is known or unknown in a given situation.

A **0-point** response shows very little or no understanding of how to define a problem.

SCORING RUBRIC FOR SHORT-ANSWER ITEMS THAT ASSESS <u>SOLVES PROBLEMS</u> (SR02):

A **2-point** response solves a problem by doing the following:
• shows understanding by organizing and using relevant information;
• uses appropriate strategies and/or procedures to construct a solution;
• provides an answer that is a viable solution, is mathematically correct, and answers the question(s) asked.

A **1-point** response does <u>one</u> of the following:
• shows partial understanding of the problem and incomplete strategies or procedures;
• uses appropriate strategies and/or procedures with a missing or incorrect answer;
• provides a correct answer with missing or incorrect work.

A **0-point** response shows very little or no understanding of how to solve a problem.

SCORING RUBRIC FOR SHORT-ANSWER ITEMS THAT ASSESS <u>MATHEMATICAL REASONING</u> (SR03, SR04):

A **2-point** response shows effective reasoning by making an appropriate interpretation or comparison, by forming and fully supporting conclusions using evidence, and/or by evaluating procedures and results.

A **1-point** response shows limited reasoning by making a partial interpretation or comparison, forming and supporting conclusions with some evidence, and/or verifying results using some evidence.

A **0-point** response shows very little or no evidence of reasoning through interpretation, comparison, reaching conclusions, supporting, or evaluating.

SCORING RUBRIC FOR SHORT-ANSWER ITEMS THAT ASSESS <u>SOLVES PROBLEMS AND REASONS LOGICALLY</u> (SR05):

A **2-point** response shows understanding of the problem, uses appropriate strategies and/or procedures, provides an answer that is a viable solution, **AND** justifies results, explains why the solution is appropriate, makes a comparison, checks for reasonableness of results, and/or validates thinking.

A **1-point** response does <u>one</u> of the following:
• shows partial understanding of the problem, incomplete strategies or procedures, an incomplete answer, AND a flawed or incomplete justification or validation.
• justifies or checks for reasonableness of results or validates thinking for a solution that is incomplete.
• shows a correct answer with missing or incorrect work.

A **0-point** response shows very little or no understanding of how to solve a problem and very little or no justification or validation.

SCORING RUBRIC FOR SHORT-ANSWER ITEMS THAT ASSESS <u>COMMUNICATES UNDERSTANDING</u>:

A **2-point** response shows understanding of how to gather, organize, and/or represent and share relevant mathematical information for a given audience and purpose.

A **1-point** response shows some understanding of how to gather, organize, and/or represent and share relevant mathematical information for a given audience and purpose; the response is not complete or is ineffectively presented.

A **0-point** response shows very little or no understanding of how to gather, organize and/or represent and share relevant mathematical information for a given audience and purpose.

SCORING RUBRIC FOR SHORT-ANSWER ITEMS THAT ASSESS <u>MAKES CONNECTIONS</u>:

A **2-point** response makes a mathematical connection, appropriately and accurately using concepts and/or procedures from two or more of the content strands, or identifies, describes, and/or creates different mathematical representations that are equivalent.

A **1-point** response shows partially correct use of concepts or procedures from two or more of the content strands, or identifies some likenesses or partially describes or creates different mathematical representations.

A **0-point** response shows very little or no use of concepts or procedures from the content strands, or does not identify, describe, or create equivalent mathematical representations.

SCORING RULES FOR EXTENDED-RESPONSE ITEMS

SCORING RUBRIC FOR EXTENDED-RESPONSE ITEMS THAT ASSESS <u>SOLVES PROBLEMS</u> (SR02):

A **4-point** response solves a problem by doing the following:
• shows understanding by organizing and using relevant information;
• uses appropriate strategies and/or procedures to construct a solution;
• provides an answer that is a viable solution, is mathematically correct, and answers the question(s) asked.

A **3-point** response shows understanding of the problem, uses appropriate strategies and/or procedures, provides an answer that follows from the student work. Calculation errors or gaps limit the viability or completeness of the solution.

A **2-point** response shows some understanding of the problem and limited use of appropriate strategies and/or procedures. The answer is a partial solution to the problem situation, is incorrect, or does not answer the question(s) asked.

A **1-point** response does one of the following:
• shows partial understanding of the problem,
• uses appropriate strategies and/or procedures with missing or incorrect answer,
• provides a correct answer with missing or incorrect work.

A **0-point** response shows very little or no understanding of how to solve a problem.

SCORING RUBRIC FOR EXTENDED-RESPONSE ITEMS THAT ASSESS <u>MATHEMATICAL REASONING</u> (SR03, SR04):

A **4-point** response shows effective reasoning by making an appropriate interpretation or comparison, forming and fully supporting conclusions using evidence, and/or evaluating procedures and results.

A **3-point** response shows moderately effective reasoning by making a partial interpretation or comparison, forming and supporting conclusions with some evidence, and/or verifying results using evidence.

A **2-point** response shows limited reasoning by analyzing some information and/or forming and supporting conclusions, or verifying results through limited use of evidence.

A **1-point** response shows faulty reasoning by incorrectly analyzing information and/or forming and supporting conclusions, or verifying results through inappropriate use of evidence or attention to inappropriate evidence.

A **0-point** response shows very little or no evidence of reasoning, analysis, interpretation, comparison, reaching conclusions, or verifying and supporting.

SCORING RUBRIC FOR EXTENDED-RESPONSE ITEMS THAT ASSESS <u>SOLVES PROBLEMS AND REASONS LOGICALLY</u> (SR05):

A **4-point** response solves a problem and shows effective reasoning by doing the following:
- shows understanding of the problem by selecting and organizing relevant information;
- uses appropriate strategies and/or procedures to construct a solution;
- provides an answer that is a viable solution to the problem, is mathematically correct, and answers the question(s) asked;
- completely justifies results, checks for reasonableness of results, and/or validates thinking and ideas.

Note: If a calculation error does not detract from the viability of the solution, the response may still earn 4 points.

A **3-point** response shows understanding of how to solve a problem and reason logically by doing the following:
- organizes and uses relevant information; uses strategies and/or procedures appropriately; provides an answer that is a viable solution to the problem, is mathematically correct, and answers the question(s) asked; and justifies results, checks for reasonableness of results, and/or validates thinking and ideas.

Note: Calculation errors or gaps limit the viability or completeness of the solution.

A **2-point** response shows some understanding of problem solving and limited reasoning by doing the following:
- shows some use of appropriate strategies and procedures with an answer that is a partial solution to the problem situation, a result of multiple errors, or incorrect **AND** shows limited reasoning when justifying results, checking for reasonableness of results, or validating thinking.

A **1-point** response does <u>one</u> of the following:
- shows little understanding of the problem, little use of appropriate strategies, concepts, and/or procedures with an incorrect or missing answer **AND** shows a flawed or incomplete justification or validation.
- shows a correct answer with missing or incorrect work.

A **0-point** response shows very little or no understanding of how to solve a problem **AND** very little or no justification or validation.

SCORING RUBRIC FOR EXTENDED-RESPONSE ITEMS THAT ASSESS COMMUNICATES UNDERSTANDING:

A **4-point** response gathers all of the applicable information from appropriate sources, organizes mathematical ideas and information in a clear and systematic manner, and/or effectively, completely, and accurately represents and shares mathematical information and ideas for a given audience and purpose.

A **3-point** response gathers most of the applicable information from appropriate sources, organizes mathematical ideas and information in a clear manner, and/or represents and shares mostly complete and accurate mathematical information and ideas for a given audience and purpose.

A **2-point** response gathers some information from appropriate sources, partially organizes ideas and information, and/or represents and shares mathematical information and ideas for a given audience and purpose with several errors and/or gaps.

A **1-point** response gathers little information from appropriate sources or related information from any source, demonstrates understandings in a manner that may be disorganized or difficult to understand, and/or represents and shares mathematical information and ideas with major errors and gaps and may or may not address the given audience or purpose.

A **0-point** response shows very little or no understanding of how to gather, organize and/or represent and share mathematical information.

In summary, mathematics items will assess whether students understand mathematical concepts and apply procedures, whether they can approach problems and develop viable solutions, whether they can reason effectively, and/or whether they can communicate their understanding effectively in mathematical terms.

GLOSSARY

acute angle: An angle that measures less than 90 degrees and greater than 0 degrees.

addition: An operation joining two or more sets where the result is the whole.

analyze: To break down material into component parts so that it may be more easily understood.

angle: Two rays that share an endpoint; classified according to the number of degrees of its measure.

approximate: To obtain a number close to an exact amount.

approximation: The result of obtaining a number close to an exact amount.

area: The area of a flat, or plane, figure is the number of unit squares that can be contained within it. The unit square is usually some standard unit, like a square meter, a square foot, or a square inch.

argument: A reason or reasons offered for or against something; suggests the use of logic and facts to support or refute a statement or idea.

associative property of addition: The sum stays the same when the grouping of addends is changed.
Example: (a + b) + c = a + (b + c); (30 + 4) + 20 = 30 + (4 + 20).

associative property of multiplication: The product stays the same when the grouping of factors is changed.
Example: (a x b) x c =
a x (b x c); (2 x 3) x 4 = 2 x (3 x 4).

attribute: A characteristic or distinctive feature.

average: A measure of central tendency; generally, average will imply arithmetic average, which could be the mean, median, or mode.

axes: Perpendicular lines used as reference lines in a coordinate system or graph; traditionally, the horizontal axis represents the independent variable and the vertical axis the dependent variable.

bar graph: A graph that uses the length of solid bars to represent numbers and compare data.

box-and-whisker plot: A graph that displays the following five points from a data set: the minimum value, the lower quartile (25th percentile), the median, the upper quartile (75th percentile), and the maximum value.

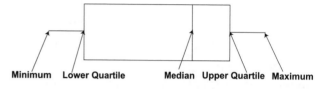

Minimum   Lower Quartile   Median Upper Quartile Maximum

chart: A method of displaying information in the form of a graph or table.

circle: A set of points in a plane that are all the same distance from the center point.
Example: A circle with center point P is shown below.

circle graph: Sometimes called a pie chart; a way of representing data that shows the fractional part or percentage of an overall set as a corresponding part of a circle.
Example:

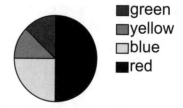

green
yellow
blue
red

GLOSSARY

circumference: The boundary line, or perimeter, of a circle; also, the length of the perimeter of a circle. Example:

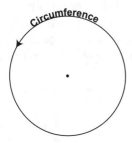

cluster: In terms of statistics, a relatively large number of data closely grouped around a particular value.

combination: A collection of objects in no particular order.
Example: The collection 1, 2, 3 is the same combination as 3, 1, 2.

common denominator: A number divisible by all of the denominators of two or more fractions.
Example: The number 12 is the common denominator of 1/2, 1/3, 1/4.

common multiple: A number that is a multiple of each of two or more numbers; used to find a common denominator when operating with fractions having unlike denominators.
Example: The number 12 is a common multiple of 2, 3, and 4. *See Multiple.*

commutative property of addition: The order in which two numbers are added does not affect the results. (The commutative property does not apply to subtraction.)
Example: a + b = b + a; 4 + 50 = 50 + 4.

commutative property of multiplication: It makes no difference in which order two numbers are multiplied. (The commutative property does not apply to division.)
Example: a x b = b x a; 3 x 5 = 5 x 3.

compare: Look for similarities and differences.

composite number: An integer greater than 1 which has whole number factors other than itself and 1. Example: Ten is a composite number because it has the factors 1, 2, 5 and 10.

conclude: To make a judgment or decision after investigating or reasoning; to infer.

conclusion: A statement that follows logically from other facts.

cone: A three-dimensional figure with one circular or elliptical base and a curved surface that joins the base to the vertex.

cones

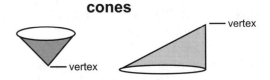

congruent figures: Figures that have the same shape and size.

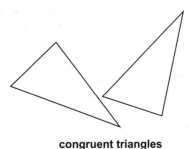

congruent triangles

conjecture: Inference or judgment based on inconclusive or incomplete evidence; guesswork.

contrast: To emphasize differences.

coordinates: Ordered pairs of numbers that identify points on a coordinate plane.
Example: (3, 4) is the coordinate of point A.

cube: A rectangular prism having six congruent square faces.

GLOSSARY

cylinder: A solid figure with two circular or elliptical bases that are congruent and parallel to each other.

data: Collected pieces of information.

decimal number: A number expressed in base 10, such as 39.456.

denominators: The number below the fraction bar; indicates the number of equivalent pieces or sets into which something is divided.

diagonal: A segment joining 2 non-consecutive vertices of a polygon.

diagram: A drawing that represents a mathematical situation.

diameter: A line segment (or the length of a segment) passing through the center of the circle with end points on the circle.

difference: The number found when subtracting one number from another; the result of a subtraction operation; the amount by which a quantity is more or less than another number.

dimensions: The length, width, or height of an object.

distributive property: The product of a number and a sum is equal to the sum of the products of the number with each of the addends in the sum. That is, for all real numbers a, b, and c in a given set, a(b + c) = ab + ac.

distributive property of multiplication over addition: A property of real numbers that states a x (b + c) = (a x b) + (a x c) where a, b, and c stand for any real numbers.
Example: 3 x (40 + 5) = (3 x 40) + (3 x 5)

dividend: A number which is to be divided by another number. Dividend ÷ divisor = quotient. Example: In 15 ÷ 3 = 5, 15 is the dividend.

$$\overset{\text{quotient}}{\text{divisor}\overline{)\text{dividend}}} \qquad \overset{5}{3\overline{)15}}$$

divisible: One integer is divisible by another non-zero integer if the quotient is an integer with a remainder of zero. Example: 12 is divisible by 3 because 12 ÷ 3 is an integer, namely 4.

division: An operation on two numbers to determine the number of sets or the size of the sets. Problems where the number of sets is unknown may be called measurement or repeated subtraction problems. Problems where the size of sets is unknown may be called fair sharing or partition problems.

divisor: The number by which the dividend is to be divided; also a factor quotient.
Example: 15 ÷ 3 = 5, 3 is the divisor.

$$\overset{\text{quotient}}{\text{divisor}\overline{)\text{dividend}}} \qquad \overset{5}{3\overline{)15}}$$

edge: The line segment formed by the intersection of two faces of a three-dimensional figure; a cube has 12 edges.

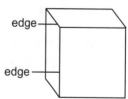

equality: Two or more sets of values are equal.

equally likely: Two outcomes are equally likely if they have the same probability of occurring.

GLOSSARY

equation: A number sentence or algebraic sentence which shows equality between two sets of values.
Example: 4 + 8 = 6 + 6, 4 + 8 = 24 ÷ 2,
4 + X = 12

equilateral: Having equal sides.

equivalent fractions: Fractions that have the same value.
Example: 3/4 and 6/8 and 9/12 are equivalent fractions.

estimate: To find an approximate value or measurement of something without exact calculation.

estimation: The process of finding an approximate value or measurement of something without exact calculation. Measurement estimation – an approximate measurement found without taking an exact measurement. Quantity estimation – an approximate number of items in a collection. Computational estimation – a number that is an approximation of a computation that we cannot (or do not wish to) determine exactly.

even number: A whole number divisible by two.
Example: 0, 4, 678 are even numbers.

event: Any subset of the sample space. In rolling a number cube, the event of rolling a "3" is a singleton event because it contains only one outcome. The event of rolling an "even number" contains three outcomes.

expanded form: A number written in component parts showing the cumulative place values of each digit in the number.
Example: 546 = 500 + 40 + 6.

experimental probability: The ratio of the number of times an event occurs to the number of trials.

exponent: A numeral written above and to the right of another numeral to indicate how many times the original number is used as a factor.
Example: The exponent "3" in 4^3 means 4 is a factor 3 times; 4^3 = 4 x 4 x 4.

expression: A combination of variables, numbers, and symbols that represent a mathematical relationship.

face: A flat surface, or side, of a solid (3-D) figure.

factor: One of two or more numbers that are multiplied together to obtain a product.
Example: In 4 x 3 = 12, 4 and 3 are factors.

figure: A geometric figure is a set of points and/or lines in 2 or 3 dimensions.

flip: Movement of a figure (or object) that reverses the figure (object).
Examples: Flipping a pancake from one side to the other. Reversing a "b" to a "d".
Tipping a "p" to a "b" or a "b" to a "p" as shown below:

fraction: A way of representing part of a whole set.
Example:

$$\frac{\text{numerator}}{\text{denominator}} = \frac{\text{dividend}}{\text{divisor}} =$$

$$\frac{\text{\# of parts under consideration}}{\text{\# of parts in a set}}$$

GLOSSARY

function machine: Applies a function rule to a set of numbers which determines a corresponding set of numbers.
Example: 9 —> Input —> Rule x 7 —> Output —> 63. If you apply the function rule "multiply by 7" to the values 5, 7, and 9, the corresponding values would be

$$5 \longrightarrow 35$$
$$7 \longrightarrow 49$$
$$9 \longrightarrow 63$$

graph: A "picture" showing how certain facts are related to each other or how they compare to one another.

greatest common factor (divisor): The largest factor of two or more numbers; often abbreviated as GCF. The GCF is also called the greatest common divisor.
Example: To find the GCF of 24 and 36:
1) Factors of 24 = {1, 2, 3, 4, 6, 8, 12, 24}.
2) Factors of 36 = {1, 2, 3, 4, 6, 9, 12, 18, 36}.
3) Common factors of 24 and 36 are {1, 2, 3, 4, 6, 12}, the largest being 12.
4) 12 is the GCF of 24 and 36.

grid: A pattern of regularly spaced horizontal and vertical lines on a plane that can be used to locate points.

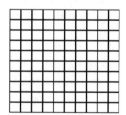

hexagon: A six-sided polygon.

regular hexagon   nonregular hexagons

histogram: A graph that shows the frequency distribution for a set of data. The graph is noted for the labels of the bars being given in intervals and for no spaces between successive bars.

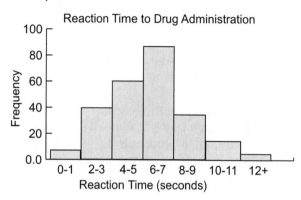

hypotenuse: The longest side of a right triangle (opposite the right angle).

identity property of addition: Adding zero to a number gives a sum identical to the given number.

identity property of multiplication: Multiplying a number by 1 gives a product identical to the given number.

improper fraction: A fraction in which the numerator is equal to or greater than the denominator.
Examples: $\frac{15}{15}$ and $\frac{5}{3}$

independent events: Two events whose outcomes have no effect on one another.
Example: The second flip of a coin is independent of the first flip of a coin.

inequality: Two or more sets of values are not equal.

interpret: To explain the meaning of information, facts, and/or observation.

GLOSSARY

intersecting lines: Lines that meet at a point.

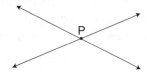

interval: Spacing of (or space between) two numbers on a number line.

inverse property of multiplication: Each non-zero real number x has a multiplicative inverse, denoted by 1/x, such that their product is 1.
Example: The number three has a multiplicative inverse of 1/3.

justify: To prove or show to be true or valid using logic and/or evidence.

least common multiple (LCM): The smallest positive multiple of two or more integers.
Example: The number 12 is the LCM of 3, 2, and 4, because it is the smallest number that is a multiple of all three numbers. 12 is also the LCM of 2, -3, 4.

line: *See undefined terms.*

line graph: A graph that uses lines (segments) to show that something is increasing, decreasing, or staying the same over time.

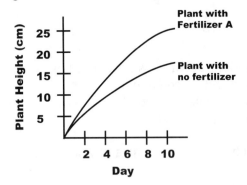

line of symmetry: A line on which a figure can be folded into two parts that are congruent mirror images of each other.

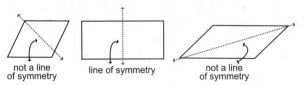

line plots: A line plot, sometimes called a dot plot, starts with a line that represents one variable. The values of the variable are labels on the line. Each observation is marked as a point above the line.

Line Plot for Quality Ratings for
Natural Peanut Butter

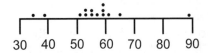

mean: A measure of central tendency found by summing the members of a set of data and dividing the sum by the number of members of the set (also called the arithmetic mean).
Example: If A = 20 children, B = 29 children, and C = 26 children, the mean number of children is found by summing the three numbers 20 + 29 + 26 to equal 75 and then dividing the sum, 75, by the number 3. So, 25 is the mean of 20, 29, 26.

median: The number in the middle of a set of data arranged in order from least to greatest or from greatest to least; or the average of the two middle terms if there is an even number of terms.
Example: For the data 6, 14, 23, 46, 69, 72, 94 —> the median is 46 (the middle number). For the data 6, 14, 23, 69, 72, 94 —> the median is also 46 (the average of the two middle numbers in the list).

method: A systematic way of accomplishing a task.

GLOSSARY

mixed number: A number expressed as the sum of an integer and a proper fraction; having a whole part and a fractional part.

Example: $6\frac{2}{3}$

mode: The item that occurs most frequently in a set of data. There may be one, more than one, or no mode. Example: The mode in {1, 3, 4, 5, 5, 7, 9} is 5.

multiple: A multiple of a number is the product of that number and an integer.
Example: Multiples of 2 = {2, 4, 6, 8, 10, 12,….}.
Multiples of 3 = {3, 6, 9, 12,….}.
Multiples of 4 = {4, 8, 12,….}.

multiplication: An operation on two numbers that tells how many in all. The first number is the number of sets and the second number tells how many in each set. Problem formats can be expressed as repeated addition, an array approach or a Cartesian product approach.

mutually exclusive: Two events are mutually exclusive if it is not possible for both of them to occur together. Example: If a die is rolled, the event "getting a 1" and the event "getting a 2" are mutually exclusive since it is not possible for the die to be both a one and a two on the same roll.

non-standard units of measure: Measurement units that are not commonly accepted as standard but are applied uniformly when measuring. Example: paperclips, pencils, cubes.

number line: A line that shows numbers ordered by magnitude from left to right or bottom to top; an arrowhead at each end indicates that the line continues endlessly in both directions; equal intervals are marked and labeled.

number sentence: An expression of a relationship between quantities as an equation or an inequality. Examples: 7 + 7 = 8 + 6; 14 < 92; 56 + 4 > 59.

numerator: The number above the line in a fraction; indicates the number of equivalent parts being considered.

obtuse angle: An angle with a measure greater than 90 degrees and less than 180 degrees.

obtuse triangle: A triangle with one obtuse angle.

octagon: An eight-sided polygon.

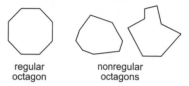

regular octagon   nonregular octagons

odd number: A whole number that is not divisible by two.
Examples: The numbers 53 and 701 are odd numbers.

operation: A mathematical process that combines numbers; basic operations of arithmetic include addition, subtraction, multiplication, and division.

order of operations: In simplifying an expression involving a number of indicated operations, perform the operations in the following order:
1. Complete all operations inside parentheses first;
2. Calculate powers and roots in the order they occur from left to right;
3. Calculate all multiplications and divisions—left to right;
4. Calculate all additions and subtractions—left to right.

Examples: 7 + 3 x 8 = 31 [multiply 3 x 8 before adding 7]; (7 + 3) x 8 = 80 [add 7 and 3 before multiplying by 8]; $7 + 3^2 \times 8 = 79$ [square 3, multiply by 8, and then add 7].

ordered pairs: Two numbers (elements) for which order is important. When used to locate points on a coordinate graph, the first element indicates distance along the x-axis (horizontal), and the second indicates distance along the y-axis (vertical).

GLOSSARY

origin: Zero on a number line or the point (0, 0) on a coordinate plane.

outcome: One of the possible results in a probability situation or activity.

outlier: A number in a set of data that is much larger or smaller than most of the other numbers in the set.

parallelogram: A quadrilateral with opposite sides parallel.

pattern: The arrangement of numbers, pictures, etc., in an organized and predictable way.
Example: 3, 6, 9 12; ♦ 0 ♦ 0 ♦ 0.

pentagon: A five-sided polygon.

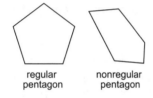

regular pentagon   nonregular pentagon

percent: A ratio of a number to 100. Percent means per hundred and is represented by the symbol %. Example: "35 to 100" means 35%.

perpendicular lines: Lines that lie on the same plane that intersect to form right angles (90 degrees).

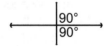

pictograph: Graph that uses pictures or symbols to represent similar data.

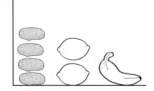

place value: The value of a digit as determined by its place in a number.
Example: In the number 135, the 3 means 3 **x** 10 or 30. In the number 356, the 3 means 3 **x** 100 or 300.

plane: *See undefined terms.*

point: *See undefined terms.*

polygons: A closed plane figure having three or more straight sides.

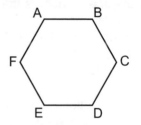

ABCDEF is a polygon.

polyhedron: A solid (3-D) figure, the faces of which are polygons.

population: A group of people, objects, or events that fit a particular description.

power: A number (exponent) representing repeated multiplication.
Example: In 3^4, 4 is a power of 3 that represents repeated multiplication so that $3^4 = 3 \times 3 \times 3 \times 3 = 81$.

precision: An indication of how finely a measurement is made; related to the unit of measurement and the calibration of the tool.
Example: Was the measurement made using a ruler marked in increments of 1/4 of an inch or, with more precision, in increments of 1/16 of an inch?

predict: To tell about or make known in advance, especially on the basis of special knowledge or inference.

prediction: A prediction is a description of what will happen before it happens. It is a foretelling that is based on a scientific law or mathematical model.

GLOSSARY

prime numbers: A whole number greater than 1 having exactly two whole number factors, itself and 1. Examples: The number 7 is prime since its only whole number factors are 1 and 7. One is not a prime number.

prism: A three-dimensional figure that has two congruent and parallel faces (bases) that are polygons; the remaining (lateral) faces are parallelograms.

probability: The numerical measure of the chance that a particular event will occur, depending on the possible events. The probability of an event, P(E), is always between 0 and 1, with 0 meaning that there is no chance of occurrence and 1 meaning a certainty of occurrence.

product: The result of a multiplication expression; factor x factor = product.
Example: 3 x 4 = 12, 12 is the product.

proportion: An equation showing that two ratios are equivalent.
Example: 2/3 = 6/9.

proportional: Constituting a proportion; having the same, or a constant, ratio.

pyramid: A solid (3-D) figure whose base is a polygon and whose other faces are triangles that meet at a common point (vertex).

quadrilateral: A four-sided polygon.
Example: ABCD is a quadrilateral.

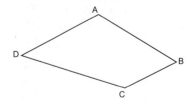

questionnaire: A set of questions for a survey.

quotient: The result of dividing one number by another number. Dividend ÷ divisor = quotient. Example: In 15 ÷ 3 = 5, 5 is the quotient.

radius: The distance from the center to the edge of a circle; or, the distance from the center of a circle to a point on the circle.

range (statistical): The absolute value of the difference between the largest and smallest values in a set of data.
Example: The range of {2, 4, 6, 7, 9, 13} is |2 – 13| or 13 – 2 or 11.

ratio: A comparison of two numbers using a variety of written forms.
Example: The ratio of two and five may be written "2 to 5" or 2:5 or 2/5.

rational number: Any number that can be expressed as a ratio of two integers, with a non-zero denominator.
Examples: Thirty-four can be written 34/1; 4.32 can be written as 432/100; 3 1/2 can be written as 7/2.

ray: A part of a line that has one end point and extends indefinitely in one direction.

reasonable: Within likely bounds; sensible.

reciprocal: The multiplicative inverse of a non-zero number.
Example: The reciprocal of x is given by 1/x.

rectangle: A quadrilateral with four right angles. A square is a rectangle.

GLOSSARY

reflection: A transformation of a figure by flipping the figure over a line, creating a mirror image.

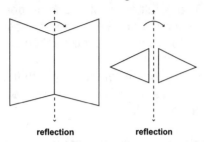

reflection   reflection

represent: To present clearly; describe; show.

rhombus: A quadrilateral with all four sides equal in length.

right angle: An angle whose measure is 90 degrees. *See Angle and Triangle.*

right circular cylinder: A cylinder whose bases are circles and the centers of whose sections form a line perpendicular to the bases.

right cylinder: A cylinder with centers of whose sections form a line perpendicular to the bases.

right triangle: A triangle having one right angle. *See Angle and Triangle.*

rotation: A transformation of a figure (or points) in a plane resulting from turning a figure around a center point O either clockwise or counterclockwise. *See Turn.*

rule: A procedure; a prescribed method; a way of describing the relationship between two sets of numbers.
Example: In the following data, the rule is to add 3:

Input	Output
3	6
5	8
9	12

sample: A portion of a population or set used in statistics.
Example: All boys under the age of ten constitute a sample of the population of all male children.

sample space: A set of all possible outcomes to a specified experiment.

scale: Sequenced collinear marks, usually at regular intervals or else representing equal steps, that are used as a reference in making measurements.

scatter plot: A graph of points (x, y), one for each item being measured, on a coordinate plane. The two coordinates of a point represent their observed, paired values.
Example: The ordered pairs may relate temperature to time of day (time, temperature).

scientific notation: A number expressed in the form of a x 10n where 1 = a < 10 and n is an integer. Examples: 342.15 can be written in scientific notation as 3.4215×10^2.
425 can be written in scientific notation as 4.25×10^2.

sequence: A set of numbers arranged in a special order or pattern.

side: A line segment connected to other segments to form the boundary of a polygon.

←side

GLOSSARY

similar figures: Having the same shape but not necessarily the same size (congruent corresponding angles and proportional corresponding sides).

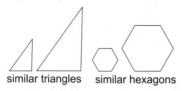

similar triangles   similar hexagons

slide: Movement of a figure that scoots the figure. *See Translation.*
Example: Scooting a book on a table.

slope: The ratio of the change in y-units (vertical) to the change in x-units (horizontal) between two points on a line.
Example: The slope of a line through (3,4) and (9,5) is 5-4/9-3 or 1/6.

solve: To find the solution to an equation or problem.

sphere: A closed surface consisting of all points in space that are the same distance from a given point (the center).
Example: A basketball.

square: A rectangle with congruent sides. *See rectangle.*

square number: An integer that is a perfect square of another integer.
Example: The number 49 is a square number because 49 is the perfect square of 7.
(i.e. 49 = 7 x 7).

square root: One of two (and only two) equal non-negative factors of a given number.
Example: Seven is the square root of 49 because 7 • 7 = 49.

standard units of measure: Units of measure commonly used, generally classified in the U.S. customary system or metric system.

Customary System:
 Length
  1 foot (ft) = 12 inches (in)
  1 yard (yd) = 3 feet, or 36 inches
  1 mile (mi) = 1,760 yards, or 5,280 feet

 Weight
  16 ounces (oz) = 1 pound (lb)
  2000 pounds = 1 ton (t)

 Capacity
  1 pint (pt) = 2 cups (c)
  1 quart (qt) = 2 pints
  1 gallon (gal) = 4 quarts

Metric System:
 Length
  1 centimeter (cm) = 10 millimeters (mm)
  1 decimeter (dm) = 10 centimeters
  1 meter (m) = 100 centimeters
  1 kilometer (km) = 1,000 meters

 Weight
  1000 milligrams (mg) = 1 gram (g)
  1,000 grams (g) = 1 kilogram (kg)

 Capacity
  1 liter (L) = 1,000 milliliters (mL)

---

stem-and-leaf plot: A method of organizing a list of numbers into stems and leaves where leaves represent units and stems represent the other digits. Stems are listed in increasing or decreasing order. Leaves are associated with their stem but need not be sequential.

Example: Ages of Adults in the Park

Data set				Stem	Leaves		
23	25	29	29	2	3	5 9 9	
36	38	39	39	3	6	8 9 9	
52	54	55	55	5	2	4 5 5	

strategy: A plan used in problem solving; such as looking for a pattern, drawing a diagram, working backward, etc.

GLOSSARY

subtraction: An operation that removes sets from an initial set, or finds the difference between two amounts when comparing two quantities.

successive events: Events that follow one another in a compound probability setting.

sum: The result of addition. Addend + Addend = Sum.

summary: A series of statements containing evidence, facts, and/or procedures that support a result.

surface area: The sum of the areas of all of the faces (or surfaces) of a 3-D object. Also the area of a net of a 3-D object. Calculations of surface area are in square units (in², m², or cm²).

survey: To get an overview by gathering data.

symbol: A letter or sign used to represent a number, function, variable, operation, quantity, or relationship. Examples: a, =, +,...

symmetrical: Having a line, plane, or point of symmetry such that for each point on the figure, there is a corresponding point that is the reflection of that point. *See line of symmetry.*

table: A method of displaying data in rows and columns.

theoretical probability: Measure of the likelihood that an event will occur; the ratio of favorable outcomes to the number of possible outcomes. Example: Knowing that there are six possible outcomes for rolling a fair number cube, one can assign the probability of 1/6 to each of the possible outcomes.

three-dimensional figure: A shape (geometric figure) having length, width, and height.

transformation (geometric): A change in position/location of a figure. Types of transformations include translation (slide), reflection (flip), rotation (turn), or combinations of these.

translation: A transformation of a figure by sliding without turning or flipping in any direction.

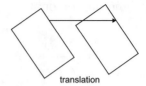
translation

trapezoid: A quadrilateral that has exactly two parallel sides; an alternate definition is a quadrilateral with at least two parallel sides. (There is no common agreement on a definition of a trapezoid).

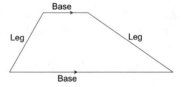
Base
Leg   Leg
Base

trend: The general direction or tendency of a set of data.

triangle: The figure formed by joining three non-collinear points with straight segments.

turn: To move a point or figure in a circular path around a center point. Motion may be either clockwise or counterclockwise. *See Rotation.* Example: The hands of a clock turn around the center of a clock in a clockwise direction.

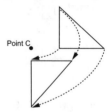
Point C

two-dimensional figure: A shape (geometric figure) having length and width. (A flat figure)

undefined terms: A term whose meaning is not defined in terms of other mathematical words, but instead is accepted with an intuitive understanding of what the term represents. The words "point," "line," and "plane" are undefined terms from geometry.

GLOSSARY

unknown: In algebra, the quantity represented by a variable.

validate: To determine, substantiate, verify, or confirm whether a given statement or argument passes specific standards.

variable: A symbol used to represent a quantity that changes or can have different values. Example: In 5n, the n is a variable.

verify: To establish as true by presentation of evidence.

vertex: A point at which two lines meet to form an angle. Where edges of a polygon or polyhedron intersect, or the point opposite the base in a pyramid or cone.

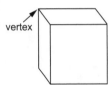

vertices: Plural of vertex.

volume: A measure in cubic units of the space contained in the interior of a solid figure. Example: The number of cubic units contained in the interior of a rectangular solid.

whole number: A number from the set of numbers {0, 1, 2, 3, 4 …}.

word forms: The expression of numbers and/or symbols in words.
Examples: 546 is "five hundred forty-six".
The "<" symbol means "is less than".
The ">" symbol means "is greater than".
The "=" symbol means "equals" or "is equal to".

***x*-axis:** One of two intersecting straight (number) lines that determine a coordinate system in a plane; typically the horizontal axis.

***y*-axis:** One of two intersecting straight (number) lines that determine a coordinate system in a plane; typically the vertical axis.

zero property of addition: Adding zero to a number gives a sum identical to the original number. Zero is the identity element of addition. *See Identity property.*
Examples: 4 + 0 = 4 and 56.89 + 0 = 56.89

zero property of multiplication: The product of any number and zero is zero.
Examples: 4 x 0 = 0 and 0 x 456.7 = 0

EXAMPLES OF COMMON TWO-DIMENSIONAL GEOMETRIC SHAPES

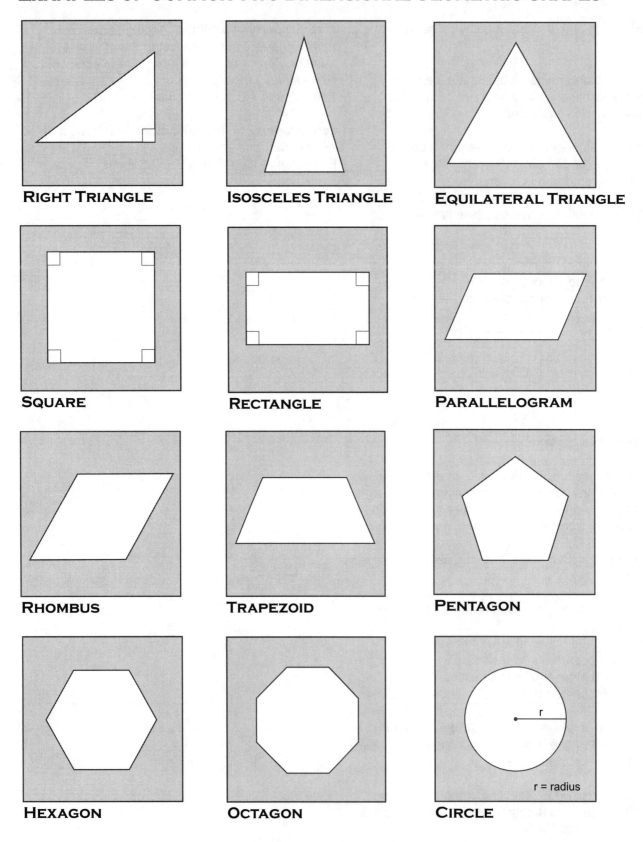

RIGHT TRIANGLE   ISOSCELES TRIANGLE   EQUILATERAL TRIANGLE

SQUARE   RECTANGLE   PARALLELOGRAM

RHOMBUS   TRAPEZOID   PENTAGON

HEXAGON   OCTAGON   CIRCLE

r = radius

EXAMPLES OF HOW LINES INTERACT

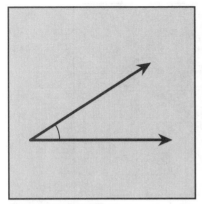

ACUTE ANGLE

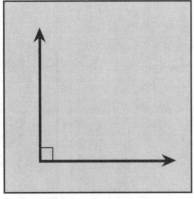

RIGHT ANGLE

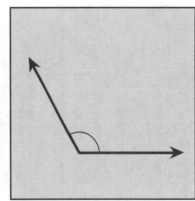

OBTUSE ANGLE

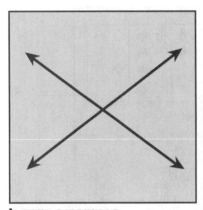

INTERSECTING

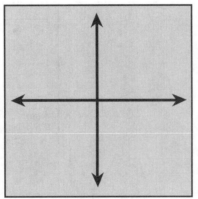

PERPENDICULAR

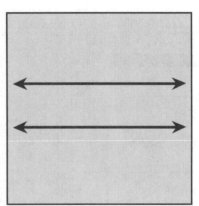

PARALLEL

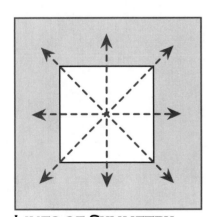

LINES OF SYMMETRY

EXAMPLES OF COMMON TYPES OF GRAPHS

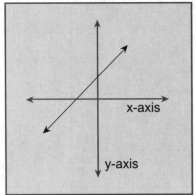
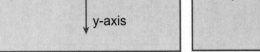

LINE GRAPH

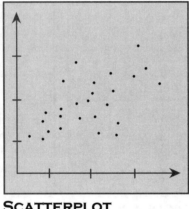

DOUBLE LINE GRAPH

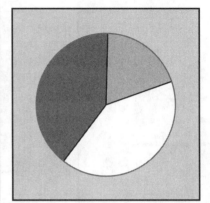

PIE CHART (CIRCLE GRAPH)

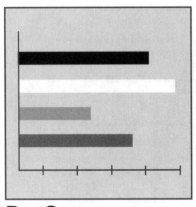

BAR GRAPH

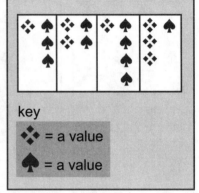

SCATTERPLOT

PICTOGRAPH

EXAMPLES OF OBJECT MOVEMENT

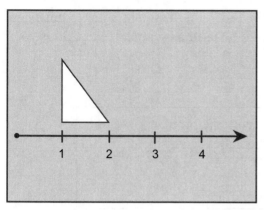 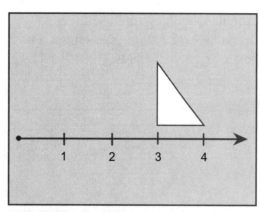

SLIDE (TRANSLATION)

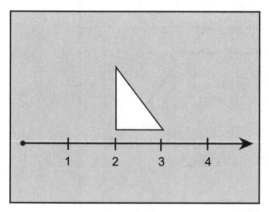 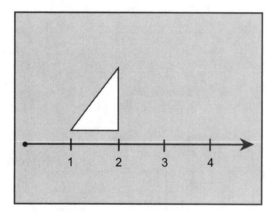

FLIP (REFLECTION)

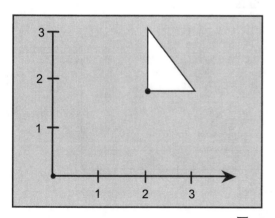 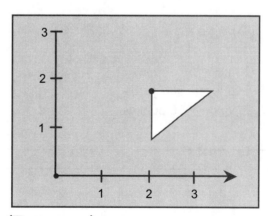

TURN (ROTATION)

FORMULA CHART

This page contains formulas you may find useful as you work the problems. You may refer to this page as you take the Mathematics Assessment. Remember, this is not to be used as scratch paper. All of your work should be written in your Mathematics Test Booklet.

Below are formulas you may find useful as you work the problems.
You may refer to this page as you take this Mathematics Assessment.

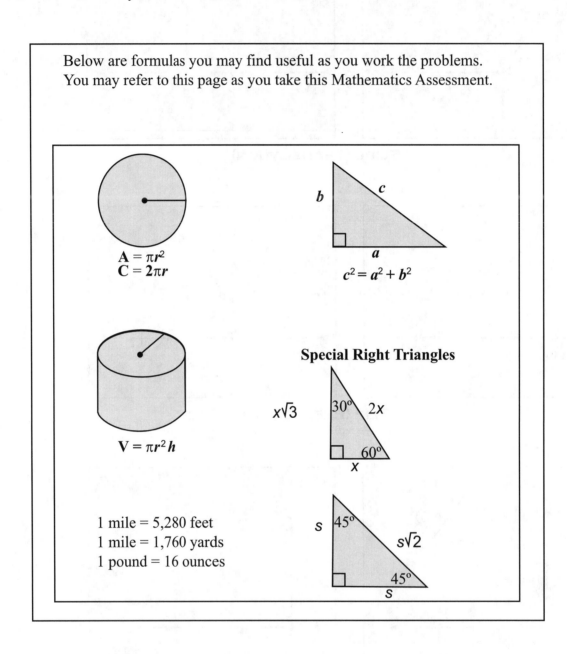

DIRECTIONS FOR MATHEMATICS TUTORIAL AND ASSESSMENTS

Today you will take the High School Washington Assessment of Student Learning in Mathematics. On this part of the test, you are permitted to use tools such as calculators, rulers, protractors, and manipulatives.

DIRECTIONS TO THE STUDENT

There are several different types of questions on this test:

1. Some questions will ask you to choose the best answer from among four answer choices. These items are worth one point.

2. Some questions will ask you to choose the best answer from among four answer choices and then tell why you chose that answer. These items are worth two points.

3. Some questions will ask you to write or draw an answer neatly and clearly inside a box.

   • Some of these questions are short. They may ask you to write an answer, to explain your thinking, draw a diagram, or show the steps you used to solve a problem. These items are worth two points.

   • Others ask for more details (graphs, tables, written summaries) or more thinking. These questions also provide you with more room for your answer. These items are worth four points.

Here are some important things to remember as you take this test:

1. Read each question carefully and think about the answer.

2. If answer choices are given, choose the best answer by filling in the circle in front of your answer.

3. If an answer box is provided, write your answer neatly and clearly **inside** the box and show all your work. Cross out any work you do not want as part of your answer. Do not use scratch paper.

4. For many items, you may have more space in the answer box than you need. You do not need to fill the whole space. Be sure to write complete answers.

5. Use only a **No. 2 pencil**, not a mechanical pencil or pen, to write your answers directly in your test booklet. If you do not have a No. 2 pencil, ask your teacher to give you one.

6. You should have plenty of time to finish every question on the test. If you do not know the answer to a question, go on to the next question. You can come back to that question later.

7. If you finish early, you may check your work in this test section **only**. Do **not** look ahead to the questions in the next section.

8. When you reach the word **STOP** in your booklet, do **not** go on until you are told to turn the page.

Sample Questions

To help you understand how to answer the test questions, look at the sample test questions below. They are included to show you what the questions in the test are like and how to mark or write your answers.

Multiple-Choice Sample Question

For this type of question, you will select the answer and fill in the circle next to it.

1   Find the missing number in the sequence below.

21, 3, 42, __, 84, 12

○ **A.** 4

● **B.** 6

○ **C.** 8

○ **D.** 9

For this sample question, the correct answer was **B**; therefore, the circle next to **B** was filled in.

Short-Answer Sample Question

For this type of question, you will write a short answer using words, numbers, or pictures.

2   The price of a hamburger drops from 75 cents to 60 cents. What is the percent decrease? Show or explain your work using words, numbers, and/or diagrams.

> The price decrease is ____20____ percent.
>
> $$\begin{array}{r} \$\ .75 \\ -\ .60 \\ \hline .15 \end{array} \qquad \frac{15}{75} = \frac{1}{5} = 20\%$$

Go on ➤

Enhanced Multiple-Choice Sample Question

For this type of question, you will select the best answer and fill in the circle next to it. Then you will tell why you chose that answer, using words, numbers, and/or pictures.

3 At Northland High School, there are 200 students. Which of the following can be answered given the information below?

> 48% of the students are male
>
> 25% of the girls are seniors
>
> 35% of the students take biology
>
> 50% of the senior girls take biology
>
> 40% of junior boys take biology

- ○ **A.** What percent of senior boys take biology?
- ○ **B.** What number of students are junior girls?
- ● **C.** What number of senior girls take biology?
- ○ **D.** What percent of the boys are juniors?

Show or explain your work using words, numbers, and/or diagrams.

48% of 200 students are male.

200 x .48 = 96 male students.

200 students - 96 male students = 104 female students.

25% of 104 female students are seniors;

104 x .25 = 26 female seniors

50% of the 26 senior females take biology;

26 x .50 = 13

13 female seniors take biology.

Go on ➤

Extended-Response Sample Question

For this type of question, you will write an extended answer, offering more examples and more detail. You may use words, numbers, and/or pictures.

4 Christine's co-workers love to eat pizza. Christine collected the following information about which kind of pizza her co-workers enjoy eating and how often during a one-month period her co-workers eat pizza.

What kind of pizza does each person like and how often do they eat it?		
Pizza	**# of Days per Month**	**Totals**
Cheese	卌 卌 卌	15
Pepperoni	卌 /	6
Sausage	////	4
Vegetable	卌 卌 卌 卌	20

Construct a bar graph using the data Christine collected. Be sure to include the following:

- an informative title

- a scale

- all the categories of subjects

- labels for the scale

- labels for the categories

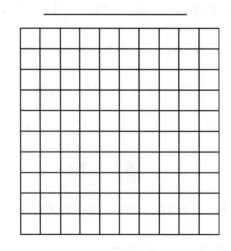

Extended-Response Sample Question

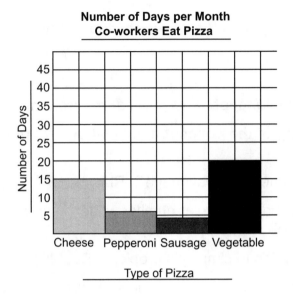

**Number of Days per Month
Co-workers Eat Pizza**

Write a question that can be answered using the information on your graph.

How many days total did Christine's co-workers

eat pizza?

Write a number sentence that answers your question.

15 + 6 + 4 + 20 = 45

Go on ➤

MATHEMATICS PRACTICE TUTORIAL

Question **1** *assesses:*

EALR 1: The student understands and applies the concepts and procedures of mathematics.

Number and numeration

Component 1.1: Understand and apply concepts and procedures from number sense.

GLE 1.1.1: Demonstrate understanding of the concept and symbolic representation of numbers written in scientific notation.

- Read and use scientific and exponential notation. [MC, RL]

- Identify a real-life situation to match a particular number written in scientific or exponential notation and justify the answer. [MC, RL]

- Use scientific or exponential notation to simplify a problem. [RL, MC]

- Illustrate the meaning of scientific notation using pictures, diagrams, or numbers. [CU]

- Read and translate numbers represented in scientific notation from calculators and other technology, tables, and charts.

> ## Vocab Review:
> cube root, equivalent, evaluate, exponent, power, property, scientific notation, square root, compare (tell how they are alike and/or different), rational number

1 Which of the following situations would be the **most** appropriate for using scientific notation?

○ **A.** Expressing the distance between cities in two adjacent states

○ **B.** Expressing the distance between cities several states apart

○ **C.** Expressing the weight of a large boulder that must be moved as part of a highway road project

○ **D.** Expressing the distance between the earth and a distant star

Go on ➤

Analysis: Scientific notation is typically used for expressing extremely large or extremely small numbers. Expressing the distance between the earth and a distant star is, by far, the most appropriate choice for using scientific notation. Choice D is correct. Choices A, B, and C are not correct because expressing the distance between cities in two adjacent states, expressing the distance between cities several states apart, and expressing the weight of a large boulder are all situations that involve much smaller numbers than the distance between the earth and a distant star.

Question 2 assesses:

EALR 1: The student understands and applies the concepts and procedures of mathematics.

Component 1.1: Understand and apply concepts and procedures from number sense.

Number and Numeration

GLE 1.1.4 Demonstrate understanding of and apply the concepts of both direct and inverse proportion.

- Explain a method for determining whether a real-world problem involves direct proportion or inverse proportion. [SP, CU, MC]

- Explain a method for solving a real-world problem involving direct proportion. [CU, MC]

- Explain a method for solving a real-world problem involving inverse proportion. [CU, MC]

- Solve problems using direct or inverse models (e.g., similarity, age of car vs. worth). [SP, MC]

- Explain, illustrate, or describe examples of direct proportion. [CU]

- Explain, illustrate, or describe examples of inverse proportion. [CU]

- Use direct or inverse proportion to determine a number of objects or a measurement in a given situation.

Vocab Review:

percent, proportion, proportional, ratio, rational number, scale, similar

2   A recent study of enrollment at a college showed that the ratio of male to female students at the school was 7:8. The total student body at this college is 600 students.

How many male students are enrolled at the college?

Explain in detail your work using words, numbers, and/or diagrams.

There are _____ male students enrolled at the college.

Go on ➤

Analysis: *For every 7 males at this college there are 8 females. There are 600 students total. Using ratio, you know that the ratio of the number of male students to the total number of students is 7:15. Create an equation to solve:* $7/15 = n/600$; $15n = 4200$; $n = 280$

*Question **3** assesses:*

EALR 1: The student understands and applies the concepts and procedures of mathematics.

Component 1.1: Understand and apply concepts and procedures from number sense.

Computation

GLE 1.1.6 Complete multi-step computations with combinations of rational numbers, including whole number powers and square roots of perfect squares, using order of operations.

- Complete multi-step computations using order of operations in situations involving combinations of rational numbers including whole number exponents and square roots of square numbers. [MC]

- Calculate using order of operations on all forms of rational numbers (e.g., (3 • 2 + 5) 2 - 8, 22 + 32).

- Use properties to reorder and rearrange expressions to compute more efficiently. [RL]

Vocab Review:

addition, difference, division, multiplication, operation, order of operations, power, product, remainder, simplify, square root, subtraction, sum, quotient, reciprocal

---

3   Which of the following is an equivalent form of $(3 \times 3)^2$?

    ○ **A.** $\dfrac{9}{2}$

    ○ **B.** 18

    ○ **C.** 36

    ○ **D.** 81

Go on ➤

Analysis: *An equivalent way to express $(3 \times 3)^2$ is 81, since $(3 \times 3)^2 = 9^2 = 81$. Choice D is correct. Choice A is incorrect because an equivalent form of this statement is 9 squared, not 9 divided by 2. Choices B and C are also incorrect. If 9 were multiplied by 2 rather than squared, the result would be 18. Finally, 9×4 is 36; 9 squared is 81.*

*Question **4** assesses:*

EALR 1: The student understands and applies the concepts and procedures of mathematics.

Component 1.1: Understand and apply concepts and procedures from number sense.

Estimation

GLE 1.1.8 Use estimation to determine the reasonableness of answers in situations involving multi-step computations with rational numbers, including whole number powers and square roots.

> • Identify when an approximation is appropriate. [MC]
>
> • Explain situations involving rational numbers where estimates are sufficient and others for which exact value is required. [CU]
>
> • Justify why an estimate would be used rather than an exact answer in a given situation. [CU]
>
> • Describe various strategies used during estimation involving integers. [CU]
>
> • Use estimation to predict or to verify the reasonableness of calculated results. [RL]

Vocab Review:

approximate (as an adjective, not a verb), approximately, approximation, estimate, estimation, evaluate, reasonable, quotient

4   Which of the following would be the **least** useful situation in which to use estimation?

     ○   **A.**   Determining the dose of medicine to be given to a hospital patient

     ○   **B.**   Determining the amount of paint required for painting a room

     ○   **C.**   Determining the length of rope needed for making leashes for two dogs

     ○   **D.**   Determining how much seed is needed to adequately re-seed a lawn

Go on ➤

Analysis: Estimation works best when there is no pressing need for precision, or in instances where being off the exact mark would make little difference to the outcome of an event. Determining the dose of medication to give to a hospital patient requires precise measurement so that the patient is not harmed, and would be the **least** useful situation of the choices for estimation. Choice A is correct. Choices B, C, and D are incorrect because determining the amount of paint required for painting a room, the length of rope needed for making leashes for two dogs, or how much seed is needed to adequately re-seed a lawn do not require precise measurements.

Question **5** *assesses:*

EALR 1: The student understands and applies the concepts and procedures of mathematics.

Component 1.2: Understand and apply concepts and procedures from measurement.

Attributes, units, and systems

GLE 1.2.1 Demonstrate understanding of how a change in one linear dimension affects surface area and volume or how changes in two linear dimensions affect perimeter, area, and volume.

- Describe and compare the impact that a change in one or more dimensions has on objects (e.g., how doubling one dimension of a cube affects the surface area and volume). [CU, MC]

- Describe how changes in the dimensions of objects affect perimeter, area, and volume in real world situations (e.g., how does the change in the diameter of an oil drum affect the area and volume). [CU, MC]

- Solve problems by deriving the changes in two dimensions necessary to obtain a desired surface area and/or volume (e.g., given a box with certain dimensions, make the volume of the box *y* cubic units by changing two dimensions of the box). [SP]

- Compare a given change in one or two dimensions on the perimeter, area, surface areas, or volumes of two objects.

- Determine the change in one dimension given a change in perimeter, area, volume, or surface area.

Vocab Review:

area, centimeter, circumference, cone, cubic units, cylinder, feet, height, inch, kilometer, meter, mile, millimeter, perimeter, prism, pyramid, radius/radii, square unit, surface area, volume, yard, compare (tell how they are alike and/or different)

5 A cardboard box with interior dimensions of 14 inches wide by 14 inches long by 20 inches high is too small to pack up a lamp.

How much more interior space is available in a box with the same width and length dimensions, and a height of 28 inches?

○ **A.** 1176 cubic inches

○ **B.** 1568 cubic inches

○ **C.** 3920 cubic inches

○ **D.** 5488 cubic inches

Explain in detail your work using words, numbers, and/or diagrams.

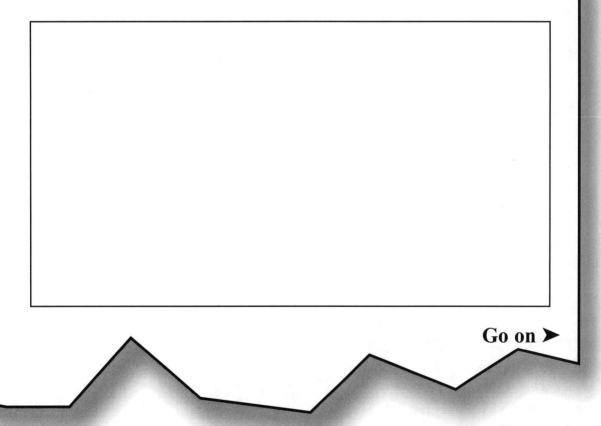

Go on ➤

Analysis: For each additional inch of height added, 196 cubic inches of volume is added: 14 inches x 14 inches x 1 inch = 196 cubic inches. Therefore, 8 more inches of height means there would be 1568 more inches of volume: 196 x 8 = 1568. Choice B is correct. Choice A, 1176 cubic inches, would be the difference in volume if 6 inches of height were added instead of 8 inches. Choice C, 3920 cubic inches, is the original volume of the box. Choice D, 5488 cubic inches, is the total volume of the larger box. The question asks how much more interior space is available, not how much total space is available.

Question **6** *assesses:*

EALR 1: The student understands and applies the concepts and procedures of mathematics.

Component 1.2: Understand and apply concepts and procedures from measurement.

Attributes, Units, and Systems

GLE 1.2.3 Demonstrate understanding of how to convert within the US or the metric system to achieve an appropriate level of precision.

- Convert within a system to a unit size appropriate to a given situation.

- Convert to a larger unit within a system while maintaining the same level of precision (e.g., represent 532 centimeters to 5.32 meters).

- Convert to a smaller unit within a system to increase the precision of a derived unit of measurement.

> **Vocab Review:**
>
> area, centimeter, circumference, cone, cubic units, cylinder, feet, height, inch, kilometer, meter, mile, millimeter, perimeter, prism, pyramid, radius/radii, square unit, surface area, volume, yard, compare (tell how they are alike and/or different)

6   Which of the following is an equivalent form of 755 centimeters?

  ○ **A.** 75.5 millimeters

  ○ **B.** 7555 millimeters

  ○ **C.** .755 meters

  ○ **D.** 7.55 meters

Go on ➤

Analysis: An equivalent form of 755 centimeters is 7.55 meters, since 1 meter = 100 centimeters; 755 cm/100 = 7.55 meters. Choice D is correct. Choice A is incorrect because an equivalent form of 75.5 millimeters is 7.55 centimeters, not 755 centimeters. Choice B is incorrect because 7555 millimeters is equivalent to 75.55 centimeters, not 755 centimeters. Choice C is incorrect because 0.755 meters is equivalent to 75.5 centimeters, not 755 centimeters.

Question **7** *assesses:*

EALR 1: The student understands and applies the concepts and procedures of mathematics.

Component 1.2: Understand and apply concepts and procedures from measurement.

Procedures and Estimation

GLE 1.2.5 Use formulas to determine measurements of prisms or cylinders.

- Explain how to use a formula for finding the volume of a prism or cylinder. [CU, MC]

- Use a formula to find the volume of a prism or cylinder. [RL, MC]

- Use a formula to derive a dimension of a right prism or right cylinder given other measures.

- Use formulas to describe and compare the surface areas and volumes of two or more right prisms and/or right cylinders. [RL]

- Use formulas to obtain measurements needed to describe a right cylinder or a right prism.

Vocab Review:

area, centimeter, cubic unit, foot/feet, inch, kilometer, meter, mile, millimeter, perimeter, Pythagorean Theorem, square unit, surface area, volume, yard, compare (tell how they are alike and/or different)

7   The formula for finding the volume of a rectangular prism is $l \times w \times h = V$. The formula for finding the volume of a square prism is $s^3 = V$. Which of the following statements best explains why the formula for finding the volume of the rectangular prism will work for the square prism, but the formula for finding the volume of the square prism will not necessarily work for the rectangular prism?

○ **A.** A square prism is a rectangular prism.

○ **B.** The width of a square prism must be a fraction of the width of the larger rectangular prism.

○ **C.** The volume of the square prism is exactly twice that of the square pyramid, while the volume of the rectangular prism is 2.25 times that of the square pyramid.

○ **D.** A rectangular prism must have a height which is different from the length.

Go on ➤

Analysis: A square prism is a rectangular prism, but a rectangular prism isn't necessarily a square prism. A square prism is just a special variety of a rectangular prism. Choice A is correct. Choice B is incorrect because it is not true that the width of a square prism must be a fraction of the width of the larger rectangular prism. It is also not true that the volume of the square prism is exactly twice that of the square pyramid, while the volume of the rectangular prism is 2.25 times that of the square pyramid. Choice C is incorrect. A rectangular prism may or may not have a height which is different from the length. Choice D is incorrect.

*Question **8** assesses:*

EALR 1: The student understands and applies the concepts and procedures of mathematics.

Component 1.2: Understand and apply concepts and procedures from measurement.

Procedures and Estimation

GLE 1.2.6 Identify situations in which estimated measurements are sufficient; use estimation to obtain reasonable measurements at an appropriate level of precision.

- Estimate quantities using derived units of measure (e.g., distance or time using miles per hour, cost using unit cost). [MC]

- Estimate derived units of measure (e.g., miles per hour, people/year, grams/cubic centimeters). [MC]

- Apply a process that can be used to find a reasonable estimate for the volume of prisms, pyramids, cylinders, and cones.

- Estimate volume and surface area for right cylinders and right prisms.

Vocab Review:

approximate, approximation, centimeter, cubic units, cube, estimate, estimation, foot/feet, gallon, gram, inch, kilogram, kiloliter, kilometer, liter, meter, mile, milligram, milliliter, millimeter, ounce, pint, pound, quart, square units, surface area, volume, yard

8 Which of the following would be the **best** estimate for the volume of a cylinder with a radius of 4.5 inches and a height of 7.2 inches?

○ **A.** 300 cubic inches

○ **B.** 500 cubic inches

○ **C.** 600 cubic inches

○ **D.** 629 cubic inches

Go on ➤

Analysis: *The actual volume would be 458 cubic inches. A quick estimate could be found by using 3 for pi, 5 for radius, and 7 for height. This would yield 525 cubic inches: $3 \times 5^2 \times 7 = 3 \times 25 \times 7 = 525$ cubic inches. Choice B is correct. Choice A, 300 cubic inches, is too low to be an accurate estimate. Choice C, 600 cubic inches, and Choice D, 629 cubic inches, are too high.*

*Question **9** assesses:*

EALR 1: The student understands and applies the concepts and procedures of mathematics.

Component 1.3: Understand and apply concepts and procedures from geometric sense.

Properties and Relationships

GLE 1.3.1 Demonstrate understanding of the relationships among 1-dimensional, 2-dimensional and 3-dimensional shapes and figures.

- Identify and label one- and two-dimensional characteristics (rays, lines, end points, line segments, vertices, and angles) in three-dimensional figures. [CU]

- Match or draw three-dimensional objects from different perspectives using the same properties and relationships (e.g., match to the correct net, draw the top view). [RL]

- Draw and label with names and symbols nets of right prisms and right cylinders. [RL, CU]

- Describe everyday objects in terms of their geometric characteristics. [CU]

- Describe or classify various shapes based on their characteristics.

- Make and test conjectures about two-dimensional and three-dimensional shapes and their individual attributes and relationships using physical, symbolic, and technological models (e.g., diagonal of a rectangle or prism is the longest interior segment; what figures make up cross-sections of a given three-dimensional shape). [SP, RL, CU, MC]

Vocab Review:

2-dimensional figure, 3-dimensional figure, acute, angle, arc, base, circle, circumference, cone, cube, cylinder, diagonal, diameter, dimensions, edge, equilateral, face, figure, hexagon, hypotenuse, intersect, isosceles, line, line segment, midpoint, obtuse, octagon, parallel, parallelogram, pentagon, perpendicular, Pythagorean Theorem, plane, point, polygon, prism, pyramid, quadrilateral, radius/radii, rectangle, rhombus, right angle, right triangle, side, square, trapezoid, triangle, figure, vertex/vertices, compare (tell how they are alike and/or different), interior angle, net, regular, tessellation, vertical angle

9   Which of the following terms **best** describes angle K?

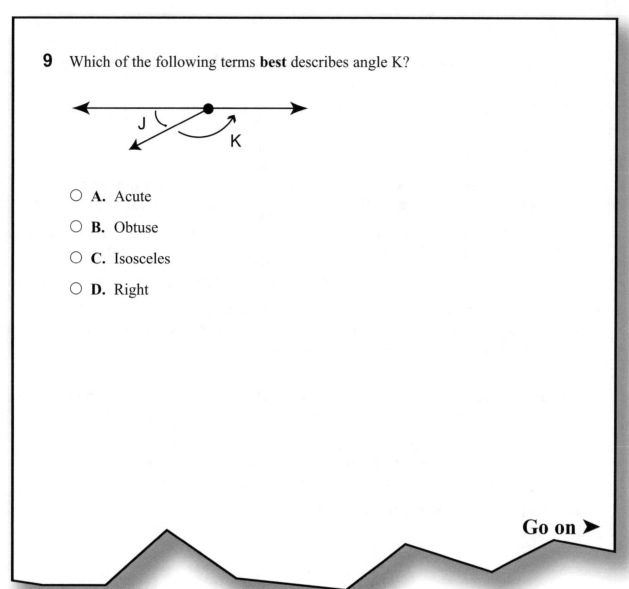

   ○ **A.** Acute

   ○ **B.** Obtuse

   ○ **C.** Isosceles

   ○ **D.** Right

Go on ➤

Analysis: Angle K is greater than 90 degrees but less than 180 degrees. An obtuse angle is greater than 90 degrees but less than 180 degrees. Choice B is correct. Choice A is incorrect because an acute angle is less than 90 degrees. Choice C is incorrect because isosceles is a type of triangle, not a way to describe an angle. Choice D is incorrect because a right angle measures exactly 90 degrees.

Question **10** *assesses:*

EALR 1: The student understands and applies the concepts and procedures of mathematics.

Component 1.3: Understand and apply concepts and procedures from geometric sense.

Properties and Relationships

GLE 1.3.2 Draw, describe, and/or compare 1-dimensional, 2-dimensional and 3-dimensional shapes and figures, including prisms, cylinders, cones, and pyramids.

- Construct geometric figures using a variety of tools and technologies (e.g., angle bisectors, perpendicular bisectors, triangles given specific characteristics). [MC]

- Draw a plane shape and justify the answer given a set of characteristics. [RL, CU]

- Use the properties of two-dimensional and three-dimensional shapes to solve mathematical problems (e.g., find the width of a river based on similar triangles; given a set of parallel lines, a transversal, and an angle, find the other angles). [SP, RL, CU, MC]

- Compare two-dimensional and three-dimensional shapes according to characteristics including faces, edges, and vertices, using actual and virtual modeling. [RL, CU]

- Use technology to generate two- and three-dimensional models of geometric figures with given geometric characteristics (e.g., generate a two-dimensional animation using pentagons with fixed coordinates for one edge). [RL, SP]

- Create a three-dimensional scale drawing with particular geometric characteristics. [SP, CU, MC]

Vocab Review:

2-dimensional figure, 3-dimensional figure, acute, angle, arc, base, circle, circumference, cone, cube, cylinder, diagonal, diameter, dimensions, edge, equilateral, face, figure, hexagon, hypotenuse, intersect, isosceles, line, line segment, midpoint, obtuse, octagon, parallel, parallelogram, pentagon, perpendicular, Pythagorean Theorem, plane, point, polygon, prism, pyramid, quadrilateral, radius/radii, rectangle, rhombus, right angle, right triangle, side, square, trapezoid, triangle, figure, vertex/vertices, compare (tell how they are alike and/or different), interior angle, net, regular, tessellation, vertical angle

10 Totem poles A, B, and C were found in a remote site by an archaeologist and

sketched nearly to scale as they stood, with pole B having toppled over onto pole A.

Measurements show that pole A is $\frac{3}{5}$ the height of pole C. Pole C is $\frac{3}{5}$ the height

of pole B. Pole A is 9 feet tall.

How tall is pole B?

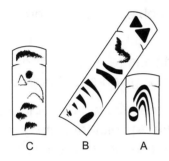

Explain in detail your thinking using words, numbers, and/or diagrams.

The height of pole B is _____ .

Go on ➤

Analysis: If pole A is 9 feet tall, and A is 3/5 as tall as pole C, then C must be 15 feet tall. Since pole C is 15 feet tall, and 15 feet is 3/5 of 25 feet, pole B must be 25 feet tall.

Question **11** *assesses:*

EALR 1: The student understands and applies the concepts and procedures of mathematics.

Component 1.3: Understand and apply concepts and procedures from geometric sense.

Locations and transformations

GLE 1.3.3 Use geometric properties to describe or identify the location of points on coordinate grids.

- Use coordinates to describe or identify the location of objects on coordinate grids.

- Describe geometric characteristics of two-dimensional objects using coordinates on a grid. [MC]

- Describe the location of points that satisfy given conditions (e.g., the set of points equidistant from a given point; a point equidistant from a given set of points). [CU]

- Represent situations on a coordinate grid or describe the location of points that satisfy given conditions (e.g., locate a gas station to be equidistant from given cities; locate a staking point to maximize the grazing area of a tethered goat). [MC, SP, RL]

- Use tools and technology to draw objects on a coordinate grid based on given conditions. [CU]

- Identify, interpret, and use the meaning of slope of a line as a rate of change using physical, symbolic, and technological models. [SP, RL, MC]

> **Vocab Review:**
> angle, axis/axes, clockwise, coordinates, counterclockwise, degrees, grid, horizontal, intersect, ordered pair, origin, parallel, perpendicular, plot, point, quadrant, reflection, rotation, transformation, translation, vertex/vertices, vertical, vertical angles, *x*-axis, *y*-axis

11   The illustration below shows points on a coordinate grid.

Which of the points lies at (-2,0)?

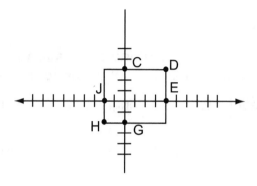

○ **A.** J

○ **B.** E

○ **C.** H

○ **D.** G

Go on ➤

Analysis: *Point J is 2 spaces to the left of the origin on the x-axis, which is located at coordinates (-2, 0). Choice A is correct. Choice B is incorrect because point E is located at the coordinates (4, 0). Choice C is incorrect because point H is located at the coordinates (-2, -2). Choice D is incorrect because point G is located at the coordinates (0, -2).*

Question **12** *assesses:*

EALR 1: The student understands and applies the concepts and procedures of mathematics.

Component 1.3: Understand and apply concepts and procedures from geometric sense.

Locations and Transformations

GLE 1.3.4 Use multiple transformations, including translations, reflections, and/or rotations, to create congruent figures in any or all of the four quadrants.

- Apply multiple transformations to create congruent and similar figures in any or all of the four quadrants.

- Use multiple transformations (combinations of translations, reflections, or rotations) to draw an image. [RL]

- Use dilation (expansion or contraction) of a given shape to form a similar shape. [RL, CU]

- Determine the final coordinates of a point after a series of transformations. [RL, CU]

- Examine figures to determine rotational symmetry about the center of the shape. [RL, MC]

- Define a set of transformations that would map one onto the other given two similar shapes. [SP, RL]

- Create a design with or without technology using a combination of two or more transformations with one or two two-dimensional figures. [SP, RL]

- Use technology to create two- and three-dimensional animations using combinations of transformations. [MC, SP, RL]

Vocab Review:

angle, axis/axes, clockwise, coordinates, counterclockwise, degrees, grid, horizontal, intersect, ordered pair, origin, parallel, perpendicular, plot, point, quadrant, reflection, rotation, transformation, translation, vertex/vertices, vertical, vertical angles, *x*-axis, *y*-axis

12   Triangle SRT is reflected over the *y*-axis along the side formed by RT and slid down one unit.

What are the new coordinates of Point S?

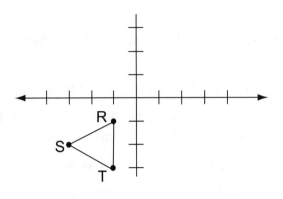

○ **A.** (3, -3)

○ **B.** (2, -2)

○ **C.** (1, -2)

○ **D.** (2, -3)

Go on ➤

Analysis: *Since the triangle's height is 3 units, point S would be at the coordinates (3, -3) when the triangle is reflected (flipped) over the y-axis by side RT and slid down one unit. Choice A is correct. Choices B, C, and D are incorrect coordinates of point S.*

*Question **13** assesses:*

EALR 1: The student understands and applies the concepts and procedures of mathematics.

Component 1.4: Understand and apply concepts and procedures from probability and statistics.

Probability

GLE 1.4.1 Demonstrate understanding of the concepts of dependent and independent events.

- Compare the probabilities of dependent and independent events. [CU, MC]

- Determine and justify whether the outcome of a first event affects the probability of a later event (e.g., drawing cards from a deck with or without replacement). [CU]

- Explain the difference between dependent and independent events. [CU]

- Explain and give examples of compound events. [CU]

Vocab Review:
compound, dependent, event, independent, outcome, probability, sample space, theoretical probability, tree diagram, combination

13 Conrad is holding six straws in such a way that the straw lengths cannot be seen. One of the straws is shorter than the rest. His three friends will each pull a straw in turn until the short straw is revealed. No straw will be replaced after it is drawn.

Which of the following statements **best** explains the probabilities involved in drawing the straws?

○ **A.** Since there are three friends and six straws, each friend will have the same probability of getting the short straw.

○ **B.** Since only one straw is drawn at a time, the person whose turn it is to draw automatically has the best odds of getting the short one on his/her draw.

○ **C.** The odds of drawing the short straw change each time a straw is drawn without the short straw being revealed, since fewer straws remain after each draw.

○ **D.** The odds cannot be determined in this kind of multiple event trial, since the short straw may be drawn at the first opportunity or on any draw after that.

Go on ➤

Analysis: The odds that the short straw will be chosen on the first draw are 1 in 6, the second draw 1 in 5, etc. The odds of drawing the short straw change each time a straw is drawn without the short straw being drawn. Choice C is correct. Choices A, B, and D are incorrect because the odds of drawing the short straw change with each longer straw that is drawn, but those odds can be determined.

Question **14** *assesses:*

EALR 1: The student understands and applies the concepts and procedures of mathematics.

Component 1.4: Understand and apply concepts and procedures from probability and statistics.

Probability

GLE 1.4.2 Determine and use probabilities of dependent and independent events.

- Generate the outcomes and probability of multiple independent and dependent events using a model or procedure (e.g., tree diagram, area model, counting procedures).

- Generate the outcomes and probability of events using a counting procedure (e.g., the number of license plates that can be made with three letters and three numbers; winning the lottery). [MC]

- Explain the relationship between theoretical probability and empirical frequency of dependent events using simulations with and without technology. [CU]

- Create a simple game based on independent probabilities wherein all players have an equal probability of winning. [MC, SP]

- Create a simple game based on compound probabilities. [MC, SP]

- Determine the sample space for independent or dependent events.

> **Vocab Review:**
> compound, dependent, event, independent, outcome, probability, sample space, theoretical probability, tree diagram

14 There are six red marbles and five blue marbles in a bag. Missy draws a red marble from the bag and does not replace it.

What is the probability of her pulling a blue marble from the bag on the second draw?

Explain in detail your work using words, numbers, and/or diagrams.

The probability of the event is _____.

Go on ➤

Analysis: The probability of drawing a red marble from the bag in the first drawing is 6/11. Once the red marble is drawn, there are only 10 marbles remaining in the bag, 5 red and 5 blue. Therefore, in the second drawing, the probability of Missy drawing a blue marble from the bag is 5/10. This can also be expressed as 0.5, 1/2, 5:10, or 1:2.

Question **15** *assesses:*

EALR 1: The student understands and applies the concepts and procedures of mathematics.

Component 1.4: Understand and apply concepts and procedures from probability and statistics.

Statistics

GLE 1.4.3 Identify possible sources of bias in questions, data collection methods, samples, and/or measures of central tendency for a situation and describe how such bias can be controlled.

- Evaluate methods and technology used to investigate a research question. [CU, MC]

- Collect data using appropriate methods.

- Use technology appropriately to collect data. [RL, MC]

- Identify appropriate data collection methods that might impact the accuracy of the results of a given situation. [RL, CU]

- Determine whether the sample for a given study was from a representative sample.

- Determine whether the methods of data collection used were appropriate for a given question or population. [RL]

Vocab Review:

bias, cluster, data, mean, median, mode, outlier, population, questionnaire, range, sample, survey, variable

15 As part of a school research project Amanda set up a table outside a local coffee and espresso bar. She wanted to find out what the average person thought of coffee prices. Amanda asked 100 people entering the store, "Do you think the price of a pound of coffee is too high, about right, or inexpensive?" She carefully marked the results as people answered and did not screen the people she asked according to age or how they were dressed. The results are shown below.

Coffee Poll	
Coffee Prices	No. of Respondents
Too High	22
About Right	61
Inexpensive	17

Which of the following **best** describes what is flawed about Amanda's coffee price research?

○ **A.** Her method of keeping results was not reliable.

○ **B.** Her sample is too small.

○ **C.** Her research question is too open-ended.

○ **D.** Her sample is likely to be biased.

Go on ➤

Analysis: Amanda's sample is likely biased. If Amanda wanted to determine what the average person thinks of the price of coffee, she should not set up a table at a place where people are likely to be coffee enthusiasts. A shopping center or theatre might be a better place to find a less biased sample. Choice D is correct. Choices A, B, and C are incorrect because there doesn't appear to be a problem with Amanda's method of keeping results, the size of her sample, or the nature of her question.

Question **16** *assesses:*

EALR 1: The student understands and applies the concepts and procedures of mathematics.

Component 1.4: Understand and apply concepts and procedures from probability and statistics.

Statistics

GLE 1.4.5 Draw a reasonable line to describe the data represented by a scatter plot and determine whether a straight line is an appropriate way to describe the trend in the data.

- Determine whether the underlying model for a set of data is linear. [RL, MC]

- Decide and explain whether it is appropriate to extend a given data set following a line of best fit. [RL, MC]

- Determine whether a linear prediction from a given set of data is appropriate for the data and support the decision with data. [MC].

- Determine whether an equation for a line is appropriate for a given set of data and support the judgment with data. [RL, MC]

- Use technology to generate data to fit a linear model. [SP, MC]

Vocab Review:

axis/axes, evaluate, intercept, line graph, origin, scale, scatter plot, trend

16   Which of the following **best** describes the data regarding Jane's ActiveWare sales?

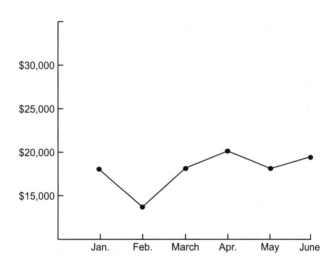

○ **A.** The data is clearly linear.

○ **B.** While the data is not exactly linear, it would be nearly linear if February were excluded.

○ **C.** Little about this data set can be determined since it is only for six months instead of a full year.

○ **D.** The reason for the decline in sales in February would need to be known before the data can fully be analyzed, or a conclusion about the data reached.

Go on ➤

Analysis: With the exception of February, sales appear to be consistently at about the $18,000 level. The data is nearly linear. Choice B is correct. Choice A is incorrect because the data is nearly, but not exactly, linear. Choices C and D are incorrect because trends can be examined for any period of time and numerical data can be analyzed without knowing the reason for changes.

Question **17** *assesses:*

EALR 1: The student understands and applies the concepts and procedures of mathematics.

Component 1.4: Understand and apply concepts and procedures from probability and statistics.

Statistics

GLE 1.4.6 Use statistics to support different points of view and/or evaluate a statistical argument based on data.

- Identify trends in a set of data in order to make a prediction based on the information. [CU, MC]

- Justify a prediction or an inference based on a set of data. [CU, MC]

- State possible factors that may influence a trend but not be reflected in the data (e.g., population growth of deer vs. availability of natural resources or hunting permits). [MC, CU, RL]

- Analyze a set of statistics to develop a logical point of view. [RL. CU, MC]

- Justify or refute claims and supporting arguments based on data. [CU, MC]

- Determine whether statistics have been used or misused to support a point of view or argument and support the evaluation with data. [RL]

Vocab Review:
axis/axes, evaluate, intercept, line graph, origin, scale, scatter plot, trend

17   In a moderately sized ocean-side community the house prices have been steadily increasing over the years. Based on tax records, the mean price for a single family home is $980,000. The median price of a single family home in this same community is $624,000.

Which of the following **best** explains this difference in prices?

○ **A.** Too many houses have been surveyed in this sample, making the sample lopsided toward the higher mean.

○ **B.** Too few houses have been surveyed in this sample, allowing the inexpensive houses to prop up the median.

○ **C.** The house market in this area is characterized by expensive houses, with some so expensive that a large gap occurs between mean and median.

○ **D.** The house market in this area is a good example of why statistics sometimes fail in practical applications, since the data indicates prices are all over the place without any way to measure them.

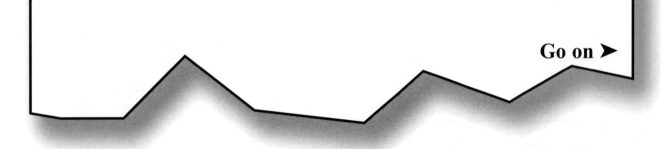

Go on ➤

Analysis: Given the choices, the difference between the mean and the median can be explained by concluding that the house market in this area is characterized by expensive homes, with some so expensive that a large gap occurs between mean and median. Choice C is correct. Choices A and B are incorrect because the data reflects the median and mean of house prices in the entire community. There is no information to indicate that the sample is either too small or too large. Choice D is incorrect because although median and mean are two ways to measure numerical data, they measure different things.

Question **18** *assesses:*

EALR 1: The student understands and applies the concepts and procedures of mathematics.

Component 1.5: Understand and apply concepts and procedures from algebraic sense.

Patterns and Functions

GLE 1.5.1 Recognize, extend or create a pattern or sequence of pairs of numbers representing a linear function.

- Identify, extend, or create a geometric or arithmetic sequence or pattern. [RL, CU]

- Translate among equivalent numerical, graphical, and algebraic forms of a linear function. [RL, MC]

- Make predictions based on a pattern or sequence.

Vocab Review:

interval, pattern, predict, rule, sequence, function

18   Identify the numerical pattern below and find the next number in the pattern.

12, 16, 32, 36, 72, 76, ____

Explain in detail your work using words, numbers, and/or diagrams.

> **The numerical pattern is _____ .**
>
> **The next number in the pattern is _____ .**

Go on ➤

Analysis: The pattern key is alternating +4, x2 to get to the next number. Since 12 + 4 = 16, and 16 x 2 = 32, and 32 + 4 = 36, and 36 x 2 = 72, and 72 + 4 = 76, the pattern can be extended to find that the next number in this sequence should be 152: 76 x 2 = 152.

Question **19** *assesses:*

EALR 1: The student understands and applies the concepts and procedures of mathematics.

Component 1.5: Understand and apply concepts and procedures from algebraic sense.

Patterns and Functions

GLE 1.5.2 Identify or write a rule to describe a pattern, sequence, and/or linear function.

- Find the equation of a line in a variety of ways (e.g., from a table, graph, slope-intercept, point-slope, two points). [RL, MC]

- Generate and use rules for a pattern to make predictions about future events (e.g., population growth, future sales, growth of corn stalks, future value of savings account). [SP, RL, MC]

- Identify or write an equation or rule to describe a pattern, sequence, and/or a linear function. [RL, CU, MC]

- Write an equation for a line given a set of information (e.g., two points, point-slope, etc.). [CU, MC]

- Write a recursive definition of a geometric pattern (e.g., Start and New = Old * Number). [CU, MC]

- Represent systems of equations and inequalities graphically. [RL, MC]

- Write a story that represents a given linear equation or expression. [CU, MC]

- Write an expression, equation, or inequality with two variables representing a linear model of a real-world problem. [CU, MC]

Vocab Review:

function, interval, pattern, predict, rule, sequence

19   Karen put $1,200.00 into a savings account that pays an annual (simple) interest rate of 6.75%.

To the nearest dollar, how much money will she have in the account at the end of three years?

○ **A.** $259

○ **B.** $1403

○ **C.** $1460

○ **D.** $1558

Go on ➤

Analysis: After the first year the account would have $1281: 1.0675 x $1200 = $1281. After the second year the account would grow to about $1367: 1.0675 x $1281 = $1367.47. After the third year the account would grow to about $1459: $1367 x 1.0675 = 1459.27. This is about $1460. The interest each year would be $81, $86.46 and $92.30. Choice C is correct. Choice A is incorrect because $259 is the amount of interest earned on the account in three years, but the question asks for the total amount of money in the account after three years. Choices B and D are incorrect because they represent calculation errors.

Question **20** *assesses:*

EALR 1: The student understands and applies the concepts and procedures of mathematics.

Component 1.5: Understand and apply concepts and procedures from algebraic sense.

Symbols and Notations

GLE 1.5.4 Use variables to write expressions, linear equations, and inequalities that represent situations involving whole number powers and square and cube roots.

- Identify and use variable quantities to read and write expressions and equations to represent situations that can be described using repeated addition (e.g., models that are linear in nature). [CU, MC]

- Identify and use variable quantities to read and write expressions and equations to represent situations that can be described using repeated multiplication (e.g., models that are exponential such as savings accounts and early stages of population growth). [CU, MC]

- Recognize and write equations in recursive form for additive models (e.g., starting value, New = Old + some number). [CU, MC]

- Recognize and write equations in recursive form for multiplicative models (e.g., starting value, New = Old x some number). [CU, MC]

- Select an expression or equation to represent a given real world situation. [MC]

Vocab Review:

algebra, algebraic, equation, expression, function, inequality, interval, power, relationship, square, square root, unknown, variable

20   Mort is 7 and he's half as old as Kim. Belinda is twice as old as Kim. Mort's age is assigned the variable *y*.

What would Belinda's age be in terms of *y*?

○ **A.** $\dfrac{1}{2}y$

○ **B.** $2y$

○ **C.** $4y$

○ **D.** y^2

Go on ➤

Analysis: *Since Mort is half as old as Kim, Kim is twice as old as Mort, or 2y = Kim's age. Since Belinda is twice as old as Kim, in terms of y, Belinda's age must be 2(2y), or 4y. Choice C is correct. Choice A is incorrect because Belinda's age is 4y, not 1/2y. Choice B is incorrect because 2y represents Kim's age, not Belinda's age. Choice D is incorrect because Belinda's age is 4y, not y².*

Question **21** *assesses:*

EALR 1: The student understands and applies the concepts and procedures of mathematics.

Component 1.5: Understand and apply concepts and procedures from algebraic sense.

Evaluating and Solving

GLE 1.5.5 Simplify expressions.

- Simplify expressions and evaluate formulas involving exponents.

- Justify a simplification of an expression involving exponents. [RL, CU]

- Use multiple mathematical strategies and properties to simplify expressions.

Vocab Review:

expression, formula, function, relationship, solve, unknown, value, variable

21   Which of the following could be eliminated as a solution for the equation $w \times e = 12$?

     ○ **A.** $w = -2$, $e = -6$

     ○ **B.** $w = \dfrac{1}{4}$, $e = 48$

     ○ **C.** $w = 2.5$, $e = 4.8$

     ○ **D.** $w = 8$, $e = \dfrac{2}{3}$

Go on ➤

Analysis: *Each of the resulting values in choices A through C either would equal 12. The equation for A would be $-2 \times -6 = 12$, which is a true statement. The equation for B would be $1/4 \times 48 = 12$, which would make the equation true. For Choice C, the equation would be $2.5 \times 4.8 = 12$, which is also true. For Choice D, however, 2/3 of 8 would clearly be less than 8, and therefore would be less than 12. Choice D is correct.*

Question **22** *assesses:*

EALR 1: The student understands and applies the concepts and procedures of mathematics.

Component 1.5: Understand and apply concepts and procedures from algebraic sense.

Evaluating and Solving

GLE 1.5.6 Solve multi-step equations and systems of equations.

- Rearrange formulas to solve for a particular variable (e.g., given, solve for *h*). [MC, CU]

- Solve real-world situations involving linear relationships and verify that the solution makes sense in relation to the problem. [SP, RL, CU, MC]

- Find the solution to a system of linear equations using tables, graphs, and symbols. [CU, MC]

- Interpret solutions of systems of equations. [CU, MC]

- Use systems of equations to analyze and solve real-life problems. [SP, CU, MC]

- Determine when two linear options yield the same outcome (e.g., given two different investment or profit options, determine when both options will yield the same result).

- Use systems of equations to determine the most advantageous outcome given a situation (e.g., given two investment options, determine under what conditions each will yield the best result). [MC, SP]

Vocab Review:

expression, formula, function, relationship, solve, unknown, value, variable

22 The formula for the circumference of a circle is C = 2π(r). Using 3.1415 as a value for π, what would be the radius of a circle with a circumference of 125.66 cm?

○ **A.** 10

○ **B.** 12

○ **C.** 18

○ **D.** 20

Go on ➤

Analysis: Plug the known information into the formula for the circumference of a circle, then solve for the radius. First, divide each side of the equation by 2π, yielding 125.66 / 2π = r; 125.66 / 6.283 = r; 20 = r. Choice D is correct. Choices A, B, and C are incorrect because using the formula to find the radius of a circle with a circumference of 125.66 cm would not result in the values in these choices.

Question **23** *assesses:*

EALR 2: The student uses mathematics to define and solve problems.

Component 2.1: Define Problems

GLE 2.1.1 Identify questions to be answered in complex situations.

- Use strategies to become informed about the situation (e.g., listing information; examine the table for patterns; create a scatter plot to look for patterns; asking questions).

- Summarize the problem (e.g., there are Olympic winning times over the past 50 years; both men's and women's times are decreasing; will there come a time when women run faster than men).

- Define the problem (e.g., if the pattern continues in the same fashion, will women run faster than men and, if so, when will that occur).

Vocab Review:

not important, not needed, relevant

23 The table below shows data for the fish caught in an annual fishing tournament founded twelve years ago.

Fish	Average Weight	Record Weight
Mahi Mahi	24.4 lbs	86.2 lbs
Black Marlin	260.7 lbs	488.5 lbs
Blue Marlin	320.0 lbs	564.8 lbs
Wahoo	31.0 lbs	91.2 lbs

This year, the 13th year of the tournament, the winning Mahi Mahi weighed 34 lbs., the winning Black Marlin weighed 312.4 lbs, the winning Blue Marlin weighed 340.4 lbs., and the winning Wahoo weighed 55 lbs.

Which fish is most likely to drive up the average weight in its category once results for the thirteenth year are included in the overall statistics?

○ **A.** Mahi Mahi

○ **B.** Black Marlin

○ **C.** Blue Marlin

○ **D.** Wahoo

Go on ➤

Analysis: The Wahoo's weight is farthest away from the mean. This year's Mahi Mahi is 39% higher than the mean. This year's Black Marlin is 20% higher than the mean. This year's Blue Marlin is about 6% higher than the mean. This year's Wahoo is about 77% heavier than the mean: 55 − 31 = 24 lbs.; 24 /31 = 77.4%. Choice D is correct. Choices A, B, and C are incorrect because the winning Mahi Mahi, Black Marlin, and Blue Marlin are not the most likely to drive up the average weight in their categories once results for the 13th year are included in the statistics.

Question **24** *assesses:*

EALR 2: The student uses mathematics to define and solve problems.

Component 2.1: Define Problems

GLE 2.1.2 Recognize when information is missing or extraneous.

- Determine whether enough information is given to find a solution (e.g., list what is needed to be found; extend the pattern to see if women's times will be less).

- Identify or clarify the question the problem presents.

Vocab Review:
not important, not needed, relevant

24 Holly wanted to determine how much money she spent for fuel for her car in a given week. On Monday she filled the tank and noted the price per gallon, the car's mileage, the amount of fuel purchased, and the total purchase cost. Holly drives quite a bit each week, so she had to fill up again on Friday. At this stop, she again recorded the price per gallon, the car's mileage, the amount of fuel purchased, and the total purchase cost.

Which of the following data is needed for Holly to find how much money she spent on fuel in that week?

○ **A.** The number of gallons purchased on both Monday and Friday

○ **B.** The price per gallon she paid on both Monday and Friday

○ **C.** The total purchase cost for both Monday and Friday

○ **D.** The amount of fuel she used from the second fill-up

Go on ➤

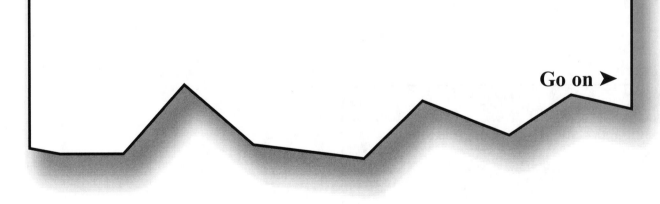

Analysis: The question asks what data is needed for Holly to find how much money she spent on fuel in that week. To answer this question, Holly needs only to add the total purchase cost for both Monday and Friday. All of the other data is extraneous. Choice C is correct.

Question **25** *assesses:*

EALR 2: The student uses mathematics to define and solve problems.

Component: Define Problems

GLE 2.1.3 Identify what is known and unknown in complex situations.

- Determine whether information is missing or extraneous (e.g., compare the list of known things to the list of needed things to see if there are things that are not needed).

- Formulate or identify additional question(s) that need to be answered in order to find a solution to a given problem.

- Identify the "known" and "unknown" information in a given problem situation.

Vocab Review:

not important, not needed, relevant

25 John delivers flowers and earns $3.00 per hour, plus tips and $0.28 per mile. He averages 200 miles per week delivering flowers. John works 30 hours per week and averages $30 per day in tips.

What additional information is needed in order to find John's average weekly income from his flower delivery job?

Explain in detail your answer using words, numbers and/or diagrams.

Go on ➤

Analysis: In order to find John's average weekly income, the number of days John works would have to be known. From the information given, the amount John earns in a week from his hourly wage and the amount he is paid in mileage can be calculated. However, his tip income for the week cannot be determined unless the number of days John works is known.

*Question **26** assesses:*

EALR 2: The student uses mathematics to define and solve problems.

Component 2.2: Construct solutions.

GLE 2.2.1 Select and organize relevant information.

> • Organize relevant information from multiple sources (e.g., create a list of known and unknown information; create a scatter plot of men's and women's times vs. time on the same coordinate axis to analyze the patterns).

Vocab Review:

solution, solve, strategy

26 Alice is preparing a dinner for friends who are coming over at 7:15 p.m. The appetizers need to be ready by about 7:25 p.m. The soup will be served around 7:50 p.m. It will require only 5 minutes to heat since it is to be served lukewarm. The main course should be ready to be served at 8:25 p.m. It's a leg of lamb which takes 1 hour 40 minutes to bake in a 380-degree oven. The dessert cake is expected to be served at 8:55 p.m. Since it has already been baked, the only preparation time is heating the cake slightly until it warms and the icing just begins to melt, which takes 8 minutes in a 250-degree oven. Alice doesn't want to forget to apply the seasonings to the lamb, which is best done after it has been cooking for about fifty minutes.

What would be the right time to apply the seasonings to the lamb in order for the timing to work out?

Explain in detail your answer using words, numbers, and/or diagrams.

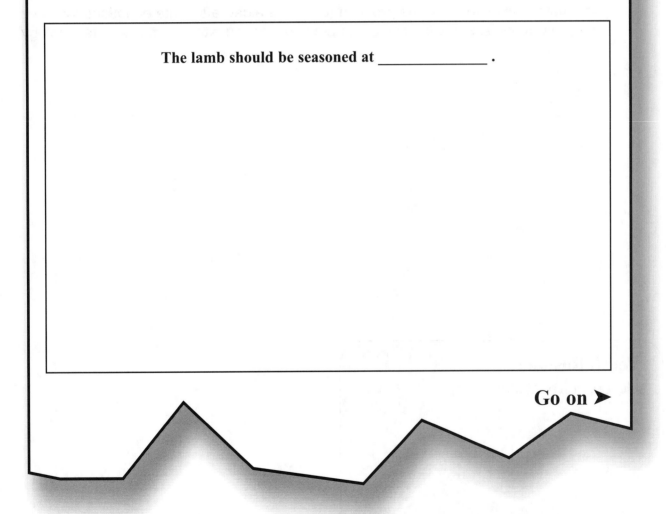

The lamb should be seasoned at _____ .

Go on ➤

Analysis: The lamb will be served at 8:25, so it starts cooking 1 hour and 40 minutes earlier, at 6:45. The seasoning should be applied 50 minutes into cooking, at 7:35 p.m.

Question **27** *assesses:*

EALR 2: The student uses mathematics to define and solve problems.

Component 2.2: Construct Solutions.

GLE 2.2.2 Use appropriate concepts and procedures from number sense, measurement, geometric sense, probability and statistics, and algebraic sense.

- Select and apply appropriate mathematical tools to devise a strategy in a situation (e.g., if the data, in either tabular or graphical form, suggest a linear relationship, plan to find a linear equation for each set of data; solve those equations simultaneously [or use technology to find the intersection of the two lines] to answer the question). If the data pattern suggests a non-linear model, plan to project what the pattern is and extend that pattern.

- Implement the plan devised to solve the problem (e.g., solve the set of simultaneous equations to arrive at a time where the two times are the same).

- Use mathematics to solve the problem (e.g., use algebra to write equations for the two linear models, solve the system of equations using either symbols or technology).

Vocab Review:
solution, solve, strategy

27   The commuter train departs every 25 minutes from Engle Station. The regular service train departs Engle Station every 40 minutes. Both trains begin service at 5:55 a.m.

What time is the next instance during the day when both trains are departing the station at the same time?

Explain in detail using words, numbers and/or diagrams.

What is the next time both trains depart?_____

Go on ➤

Analysis: The trains' run times have a common multiple at 3 hours, 20 minutes. Therefore, the next time both trains will depart the station will be 3 hours 20 minutes later, or 9:15 am.

*Question **28** assesses:*

EALR 2: The student uses mathematics to define and solve problems.

Component 2.2: Construct Solutions.

GLE 2.2.3 Use a variety of strategies and approaches.

- Identify when an approach is unproductive and modify or try a new approach (e.g., if the result does not make sense in the context, return to the plan to see if something has gone wrong and adjust accordingly).

Vocab Review:

solution, solve, strategy

28   A college medical center offered flu shots to students as an option for flu prevention. After the flu season, the center surveyed all students enrolled at the college, asking the question, "Did you have the flu during the past flu season?" Fifty-six percent of the respondents replied, "Yes." The college concluded that the flu shots had not been effective and decided not to offer them the following year.

Was the approach the medical center took in order to reach this conclusion valid?

Explain in detail your answer using words, numbers, and/or diagrams.

Go on ➤

Analysis: *The decision is not valid. Some students received the shot and others did not. Because ALL students were surveyed and the survey data represented the percentage (56%) of ALL students who had contracted the flu, rather than the percentage of students who contracted the flu after receiving a flu shot, it was a faulty decision to base continuation of the flu shot option on the result of this survey.*

Question **29** *assesses:*

EALR 2: The student uses mathematics to define and solve problems.

Component 2.2: Construct Solutions.

GLE 2.2.4 Determine whether a solution is viable, mathematically correct, and answers the question(s) asked.

- • Check the solution to see if it works (e.g., the solution may be a partial year [i.e., 2003.6]; decide how to deal with this and also if the year is reasonable [i.e., 1925 does not make sense given the context]).

Vocab Review:
solution, solve, strategy

29   While taking a test, Pat, Judd, Don, and Steve were all trying to identify the approximate sum of $\sqrt{17}$ and $2\sqrt{31}$. Their estimates and their lines of initial reasoning are shown below.

Which student's estimation is incorrect?

   ○ **A.** Pat's answer: 15.259; Pat reasoned, "I used a calculator, then rounded."

   ○ **B.** Don's answer: 15; Don reasoned, " $\sqrt{17}$ is about 4; $\sqrt{31}$ is halfway between $\sqrt{25}$ which is 5, and $\sqrt{36}$, which is 6, so $\sqrt{31}$ is about 5.5."

   ○ **C.** Judd's answer: 14; Judd reasoned, " $\sqrt{17}$ is about 4; $\sqrt{31}$ is about 5."

   ○ **D.** Steve's answer: 12; Steve reasoned, " $\sqrt{17}$ is about 4; $2 \times 31 = 62$ and $\sqrt{62}$ is about 8."

Go on ➤

Analysis: Judd's and Don's lines of reasoning were similar and correct, although Judd underestimated more than Don did. Pat's use of a calculator provided a better estimate, since she knew at least 5 or 6 decimal places. Steve moved the 2 under the radical sign where it became the square root of 2 and lost its identity as a whole number. (The square root of 2 equals 1.414...) This is not correct. Steve is the student who did not estimate correctly. Choice D is correct.

Question **30** *assesses:*

EALR 3: The student uses mathematical reasoning.

Component 3.1: Analyze information.

GLE 3.1.1. Interpret, compare, and integrate mathematical information from multiple sources.

- Use the properties of two-dimensional and three-dimensional figures to solve mathematical problems (e.g., find the width of a river based on similar triangles; given a set of parallel lines, a transversal, and an angle, find the other angles).

- Interpret mathematical information or results.

- Compare mathematical information in text, graphs, tables, diagrams, and/or pictorial representations.

- Compare information in order to answer a question.

- Identify the agreement (or differences) between information, diagrams, and/or pictorial representations.

- Compare patterns or trends shown by data or other information.

- Integrate information from two or more sources to develop an interpretation.

Vocab Review:

agree, analyze, compare (tell how they are alike and/or different), interpret

30   Line J and Line E are parallel. Angle N measures 40 degrees. What is the measure of angle M?

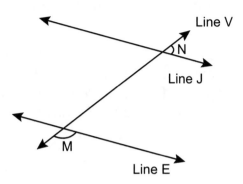

   ○   **A.**   120 degrees

   ○   **B.**   140 degrees

   ○   **C.**   160 degrees

   ○   **D.**   40 degrees

Go on ➤

Analysis: Since Lines J and E are parallel, angles N and M must be complementary angles. This means that when the measures of the angles are added together, the total must be 180 degrees. Therefore, if angle N measures 40 degrees, angle M must measure 180 degrees – 40 degrees, or 140 degrees. Choice B is correct. Choice A is incorrect because angle N is 40 degrees, not 60 degrees. Choice C is incorrect because angle N is 40 degrees, not 20 degrees. Choice D is incorrect because angle N is 40 degrees; therefore, its complementary angle is 140 degrees.

Question **31** *assesses:*

EALR 3: The student uses mathematical reasoning.

Component 3.2: Conclude.

GLE 3.2.1 Draw conclusions and support them using inductive and deductive reasoning.

- Make and test conjectures about two-dimensional and three-dimensional figures and their individual attributes and relationships using physical, symbolic, and technological models (e.g., diagonal of a rectangle or prism is the longest interior segment; what figures make up cross-sections of a given three-dimensional shape).

Vocab Review:

analyze, conclude, conclusion, evaluate, justify, prove, support, verify

31   The illustration below shows a standard cone.

Which of the following would be a cross section if the cone were cut as indicated by the dotted line?

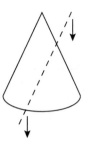

○ **A.**

○ **B.**

○ **C.**

○ **D.**

Go on ➤

Analysis: *This standard cone has been cut across the shoulder down through the base. Choice B is the only choice that depicts the cone's flat base. Choice B is correct. Since the base of a cone is flat, Choices A, C, and D can be ruled out because they all have curved bottoms.*

Question **32** *assesses:*

EALR 3: The student uses mathematical reasoning.

Component 3.2: Conclude

GLE 3.2.2 Evaluate procedures and make needed revisions.

- Evaluate procedures used and/or the results based on a given partial or complete solution to a problem.

- Compare and describe the volume of cylinders, cones, and prisms when an attribute is changed (e.g., the area of the base, the height of a solid).

- Draw a plane shape of a given set of characteristics and justify the answer.

- Identify trends in a set of data in order to make a prediction based on the information.

- Use statistics to support different points of view.

- Examine claims and supporting arguments based on data and make needed revisions.

Vocab Review:

analyze, conclude, conclusion, evaluate, justify, prove, support, verify

32 To the nearest cubic inch, how much volume is present for every inch of height in a standard cylinder with a radius of 7.5 inches? Use 3.1415 as an estimate for π.

    ○ **A.** 56 cubic inches

    ○ **B.** 137 cubic inches

    ○ **C.** 156 cubic inches

    ○ **D.** 177 cubic inches

Go on ➤

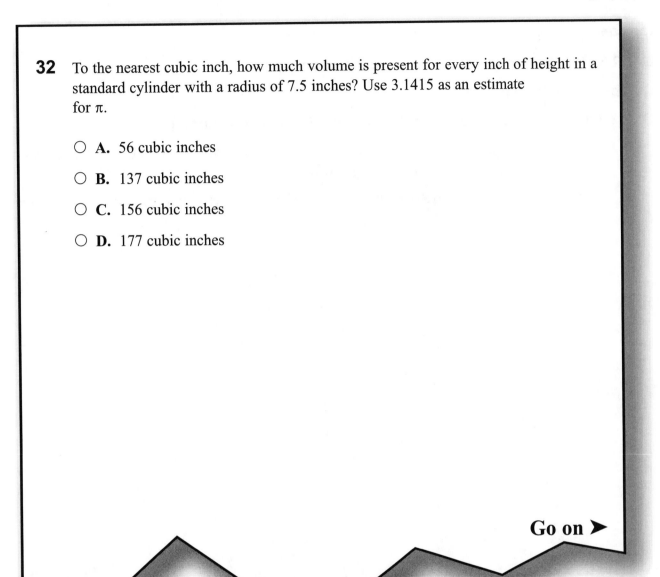

Analysis: There would be approximately 177 cubic inches in volume for every inch of height in a standard cylinder with radius of 7.5 inches, since $V = 3.1415(7.5)^2 = 3.1415(56.25) = 176.70$. Choice D is correct. Choice A, 56 cubic inches, is incorrect since it is the radius squared and needs to be multiplied by π. Choices B and C can be ruled out because they do not represent enough volume.

Question **33** *assesses:*

EALR 3: The student uses mathematical reasoning.

Component 3.3: Verify results.

GLE 3.3.1 Justify results using inductive and deductive reasoning.

- Compare and contrast similar two-dimensional figures and shapes using properties of two-dimensional figures and shapes. (1.3.2)

- Find a reasonable estimate for the volume of prisms, pyramids, cylinders, and cones. (1.2.6)

Vocab Review:

conclusion, justify, solution, solve, strategy, support, validate

33 Karen wants to gift wrap a carton that measures 18" x 12" x 5". A gift shop has rolls of wrapping paper that are 30" wide with a total area of 30 ft². The shop also carries rolls that are 36" wide, with a total area of 85 ft².

Which type of wrapping paper should Karen buy?

Explain in detail your answer using words, numbers, and/or diagrams.

Go on ➤

Analysis: *The surface area of the carton is 2(18 x 12) + 2(18 x 5) + 2(12 x 5) = 732 sq. inches. Because 144 square inches equal one square foot, 732 must be divided by 144 to convert square inches to square feet: 732 sq. in. ÷ 144 sq. in. = 5.08 sq. ft. of paper needed. The paper that is 30" wide has an area of 30 square feet, so it will cover the carton and there will be less paper left over than if the larger roll is used.*

Question **34** *assesses:*

EALR 3: The student uses mathematical reasoning.

Component 3.3: Verify results.

GLE 3.3.2 Check for reasonableness of results.

- Items may ask students to use various concepts, procedures, and problem-solving strategies to construct a solution for a given situation and then to check for reasonableness of results.

Vocab Review:

conclusion, justify, solution, solve, strategy, support, validate

34 Below is a rainfall chart for Roswell, NM, recorded for the current year.

Month	January	February	March	April	May	June	July
# of Inches	1.05	.88	.55	.65	.19	1.20	.05

Researching Roswell, New Mexico, you found that the annual rainfall over a 20-year span averaged 2.44 inches, with little rainfall coming during the summer months. What conclusion could most reasonably be drawn from the table?

Explain in detail your answer using words, numbers, and/or diagrams.

○ **A.** A mistake must have been made recording at least several of the rainfall entries.

○ **B.** Only the entry for June is a mistake; the rest of the months match what would be expected.

○ **C.** The entries are correct. It is simply a wetter than normal year, which would have little impact on the average rainfall amounts recorded over two decades.

○ **D.** While the data for this year certainly appears irregular, no conclusion can be drawn based on what is known.

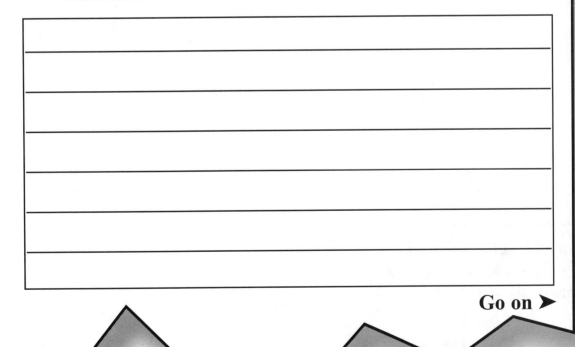

Go on ➤

Analysis: There is no evidence to support that any mistake was made in the recording of the data. Also, without data for individual years, it is impossible to know how this year compares to a typical year's rainfall. Choices A, B, and C are incorrect. No conclusion can be drawn based on what is known. Choice D is correct.

Question **35** *assesses:*

EALR 3: The student uses mathematical reasoning.

Component 3.3: Verify results.

GLE 3.3.3 Validate thinking and mathematical ideas using models, known facts, patterns, relationships, counter examples, and/or proportional reasoning.

- Examine a set of data, research other sources to see if the data is consistent, find articles written to see if the data makes sense, to develop a logical point of view and to support that view.

Vocab Review:
conclusion, justify, solution, solve, strategy, support, validate

35 Write an equation of a line that could be drawn to represent the points shown on the graph below.

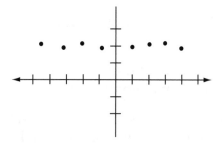

Explain in detail your answer using words, numbers, and/or pictures.

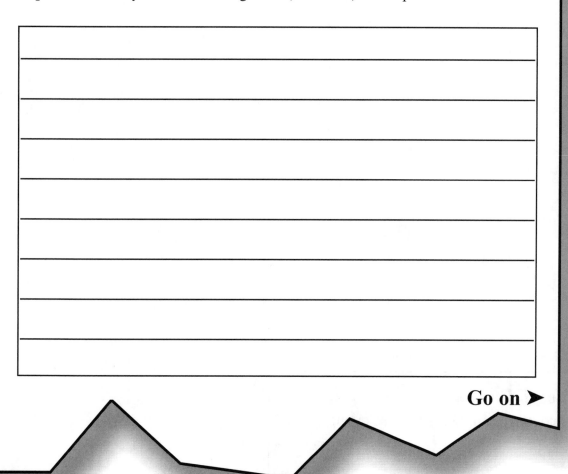

Go on ➤

Analysis: *The data points suggest a line at $y = 2$ because all of the points are located in the vicinity of $y = 2$.*

Question **36** *assesses:*

EALR 4: The student communicates knowledge and understanding in both everyday and mathematical language.

Component 4.1: Gather information.

GLE 4.1.1 Develop or select and follow an efficient system for collecting mathematical information for a given purpose.

- List or describe the general procedure/order of steps of a plan to gather exactly the information sought and no irrelevant information.

- Collect data efficiently on the outcomes of first events and later events to determine and justify how the first event affects the probability of later events (e.g., drawing cards from a deck with or without replacement).

Vocab Review:

irrelevant, plan, procedure, relevant

36 Which of the following steps would come first when collecting data for a research project?

○ **A.** Analyze the data.

○ **B.** Select a sample group.

○ **C.** Determine a method for recording the data, such as pencil and paper.

○ **D.** Develop a plan to deal with describing the results of the research, and ways to defend the results.

List all **four** steps in the order in which they would be completed.

Explain in detail your answer using words, numbers, and/or diagrams.

Go on ➤

Analysis: Selecting a sample group is the first step for collecting data for a research project. Choice B is correct. The next steps in order are as follows: determining a method for recording the data (C); analyzing the results (A); and developing a plan to deal with the results (D).

Question 37 assesses:

EALR 4: The student communicates knowledge and understanding in both everyday and mathematical language.

Component 4.1: Gather information.

GLE 4.1.2 Extract mathematical information for a given purpose from multiple, self-selected sources using reading, listening, and/or observation.

- Extract and explain or describe mathematical information from various sources such as pictures, symbols, text, tables, charts, graphs, diagrams, and models.

- Write questions that could be answered using data sources such as magazines, newspapers, menus, sales and travel brochures, TV and bus schedules, or sales receipts.

- State possible factors that may influence a trend but not be reflected in the data (e.g., population growth of deer vs. availability of natural resources or hunting permits).

Vocab Review:

irrelevant, plan, procedure, relevant

37 Elmer found that by running his car at no more than 40 mph on his way to work, his gas mileage improved by 30% over running his car at about 60 mph. Elmer is considering dropping the maximum mph to 20, and hopes to save another 30% in fuel.

Which of the following **best** describes what would happen if he reduced his maximum speed to 20 mph?

○ **A.** The cost of fuel may rise while he is trying his experiment.

○ **B.** The cost of fuel may decline while he is trying his experiment.

○ **C.** The engine will be inefficient at those lower speeds, eliminating the fuel savings.

○ **D.** While driving more slowly tends to save fuel, it also takes more time, which may represent a non-mathematical factor in why Elmer cannot slow his speed any further.

Explain in detail using words, numbers, and/or diagrams.

Go on ➤

Analysis: While driving more slowly tends to save fuel, it also takes more time, which may represent a non-mathematical factor in why Elmer cannot slow his speed any further. The time required represents a factor that may influence this trend but is not reflected in his preliminary fuel savings data. Choice D is correct. Choices A and B are incorrect because this question deals with fuel consumption, not the cost of the fuel. Choice C is incorrect because not enough information is known about the efficiency of his engine to make this determination.

Question **38** *assesses:*

EALR 4: The student communicates knowledge and understanding in both everyday and mathematical language.

Component 4.2: Organize, represent, and share information.

GLE 4.2.1 Organize, clarify, and refine mathematical information relevant to a given purpose.

- Explain or represent mathematical information using pictures, tables, graphs, 2- or 3-dimensional drawings, or other appropriate forms including titles and labels, appropriate and consistent scale(s), and accurate data display for a given audience and/or purpose.

- Develop an argument to support a given point of view and set of statistics.

Vocab Review:

audience, organize, Venn Diagram

38 A soft drink company began with sales of $120,000 in its first year, growing steadily in the next three years until sales reached $405,000. Sales at the end of the fifth year grew to $810,000.

Describe the growth in a mathematical sense.

Explain in detail your answer using words, numbers, and/or diagrams.

Go on ➤

Analysis: The pattern of growth from years 1 to 4 is 50% each year. In year 1, sales were $120,000. In year 2, sales could have been 50% higher, or $180,000. In year 3, sales again could have been 50% higher than in year 2, or about $270,000. After year 4, sales, we know, were 50% higher than $270,000, or $405,000. In the last year, sales from the previous year doubled from $405,000 to $810,000.

Question **39** *assesses:*

EALR 4: The student communicates knowledge and understanding in both everyday and mathematical language.

Component 4.2: Organize, represent, and share information.

GLE 4.2.2 Use everyday and mathematical language and notation in appropriate and efficient forms to clearly express or represent complex ideas and information.

- Explain how division of measurements produces a derived unit of measurement (e.g., miles traveled divided by hours traveled yields the derived unit [miles per hour]).

- Describe the location of points that satisfy given conditions (e.g., the set of points equidistant from a given point; a point equidistant from a given set of points).

- Describe and compare the impact that a change in one or more dimensions has on objects (e.g., doubling the edge of a cube affects the surface area).

- Explain the relationship between theoretical probability and empirical frequency of dependent events using simulations with and without technology.

Vocab Review:
audience, organize, Venn Diagram

39 Cory mows grass to earn extra money. He has found that a yard which measures roughly 100 feet by 200 feet can be mowed in about a half hour. That size yard is his basic pricing unit and he quotes new jobs based on this. For a yard this size, Cory supplies the lawnmower, provides gas for the job, and charges ten dollars.

Create a derived unit of measure that accurately describes this situation.

Explain in detail your answer using words, numbers, and/or diagrams.

Go on ➤

Analysis: The charge for a single "yard unit" is for one lawn, which takes 30 minutes. The charge for mowing this lawn is $10, which would equate to $20 an hour: 2 x $10 = $20/hour. Other ways to describe this situation include: two yard units per hour; one yard unit per half hour; and one yard unit per ten dollars.

Question **40** *assesses:*

EALR 4: The student communicates knowledge and understanding in both everyday and mathematical language.

Component 4.2: Organize, represent, and share information.

GLE 4.2.3 Explain and/or represent complex mathematical ideas and information in ways appropriate for audience and purpose in a context that is relevant to tenth grade students.

- Clearly explain or represent mathematical information using pictures, tables, graphs, 2- or 3-dimensional drawings, or other appropriate forms including titles and labels, appropriate and consistent scale(s), and accurate data display for a given audience and/or purpose.

- Clearly explain or describe mathematical ideas, facts, properties, procedures, or strategies in a way that is appropriate for a given audience and/or purpose using mathematical language and notation.

Vocab Review:

audience, organize, Venn Diagram

40 An archer raises his bow and shoots a decoy. The path of the falling decoy is perpendicular to the ground.

What geometric figure might best be drawn to simplify solving a problem related to the distance from bow to decoy?

Explain in detail your answer using words, numbers, and/or diagrams.

Go on ➤

Analysis: The geometric figure is a right triangle. Use three points to represent the bow (B), the decoy (D), and the point where the decoy hits the ground (G). Place them in position, as described in the problem statement. Point G is directly below point D, and a vertical line segment connects the two points. Somewhere on that line segment is a point (R) that is on a horizontal line segment with point B. When R is connected to B, B to D, and D to R, a right triangle is formed, with the segment from B to D as hypotenuse (distance from bow to decoy). Point G is not one of the points that creates the triangle because the point at which the arrow is fired is higher than the ground due to the height of the archer.

Question **41** *assesses:*

EALR 5: The student understands how mathematical ideas connect within mathematics, to other subject areas, and to real-life situations.

Component 5.1: Relate concepts and procedures within mathematics.

GLE 5.1.1 Use concepts and procedures from two or more of the mathematics content strands in a given problem or situation.

- Identify which of four mathematical models or representations is equivalent to the given mathematical model or representation.

- Estimate derived units of measure (e.g., miles per hour, people/year, grams/cubic centimeters).

- Determine the final coordinates of a point after a series of transformations.

Vocab Review:
equivalent, model, relationship, represent

41   A gasoline-electric hybrid car went 545.4 miles on 11.89 gallons of gas before it needed to be refueled.

About how many miles per gallon did the hybrid get?

○ A. 40

○ B. 45

○ C. 50

○ D. 55

Go on ➤

Analysis: Using the answer choices, it is not necessary to do the decimal computation since a quick inspection of Choice A, 12 gallons x 40 = 480, and Choice C, 12 x 50 = 600, yields a range substantially above and below 545. The miles per gallon should be somewhere between 40 and 50, or about 45. Choice B is correct. Choices A, C, and D are incorrect because the value in Choice A would yield a range substantially less than 545, and the values in Choices C and D would yield a range substantially higher than 545.

Question **42** *assesses:*

EALR 5: The student understands how mathematical ideas connect within mathematics, to other subject areas, and to real-life situations.

Component 5.1: Relate concepts and procedures within mathematics.

GLE 5.1.2 Relate and use different mathematical models and representations of the same situations.

- Identify, interpret, and use the meaning of slope of a line as a rate of change using concrete, symbolic, and technological models.

- Construct one-dimensional, two-dimensional, and three-dimensional geometric figures using a variety of tools and technologies (e.g., angle bisectors, perpendicular bisectors, triangles given specific characteristics).

- Find the equation of a line in a variety of ways (e.g., from a table, graph, slope-intercept, point-slope, two points).

- Find the solution to a system of linear equations using tables, graphs and symbols.

Vocab Review:
equivalent, model, relationship, represent

42   What is the equation of a line that passes through the points (-4, 0) and (-4, -3)?

○ **A.** $x = 0$

○ **B.** $x = -3$

○ **C.** $x = -4$

○ **D.** $y = \dfrac{3}{4}x - 1$

STOP

Analysis: Notice both of the x-coordinates are the same. Since they are the same, you should recognize that this equation should be one of a vertical line passing through -4. The equation for this line is x = -4. Choice C is correct. The equations in Choices A, B, and D are incorrect because they are not equations of lines that would pass through the points (-4, 0) and (-4, -3).

MATHEMATICS ASSESSMENT ONE—SESSION ONE

On this part of the test you are permitted to use tools such as a calculator, rulers, and manipulatives.

Turn to page 69 to read the Directions for Session One of this Assessment. Then turn back to this page to begin.

1   Which of the following is the correct meaning for 4^5?

○ **A.** It's another way of expressing $4 \times 5 = \square$

○ **B.** It's another way of expressing $4 \times 4 \times 4 \times 4 \times 4 = \square$

○ **C.** It's another way of expressing $(4 \times 5) \times (4 \times 5) \times (4 \times 5) \times (4 \times 5) \times (4 \times 5) = \square$

○ **D.** It's another way of expressing $5 \times 5 \times 5 \times 5 = \square$

2   Which of the following would be the correct number to use to eliminate $\dfrac{7}{3}$ from one side of an equation using multiplication as a tool for simplifying the equation?

○ **A.** 3

○ **B.** 7

○ **C.** $\dfrac{3}{7}$

○ **D.** $-\dfrac{7}{3}$

Go on ➤

3   Simplify the expression $4^3 + 5 \times 7 - 16$.

Explain in detail your work using words, numbers, and/or diagrams.

4   Jose likes to estimate grocery store purchases by rounding the prices of items put into the shopping cart to the nearest dollar, and keeping a mental tally of this total.

Which of the following statements **best** describes Jose's estimation strategy in a practical sense?

○ **A.** It is not useful since an exact amount total cannot be computed in this way.

○ **B.** It is not useful since items with prices such as $1.55 and $ 2.44 will be rounded in opposite directions to the nearest dollar, making even a reasonable estimate unlikely.

○ **C.** It is useful since the estimate will always be higher than the actual amount owed, making it impossible to be cheated by the grocery store.

○ **D.** It is useful since this mental tally should be reasonably close to the actual amount owed.

Go on ➤

5 A field that is rectangular in shape, measuring 200 feet wide by 600 feet long, will have its width increased by 50% before the next planting season.

By what percent will the field's useable area increase?

Explain in detail your work using words, numbers, and/or diagrams.

6 Rhonda has been making a wooden deck for her house and has been cutting the pieces of wood by measuring to the nearest 1/8 of an inch. She's finding that some of the boards are ending up too long, while others are ending up too short, creating waste in materials and lost time.

Which of the following steps would **most** likely solve her problem?

- ○ **A.** Measure precisely to within 1/4 inch and make cuts based on that system of measure.

- ○ **B.** Measure precisely to within 1/16 inch and make cuts based on that system of measure.

- ○ **C.** Measure to the nearest 1/8 inch, since estimation will yield a good mix of lengths for the boards.

- ○ **D.** Move to a system of metric measure based on whole centimeters, since metrics are more precise.

Go on ➤

7   Using the formula $V = \pi r^2 h$, determine the volume of a cylinder with a height of 12 cm and a radius of 6 cm to the nearest whole number. Use 3.1415 as a value for π.

○ **A.** 226 cubic cm

○ **B.** 1357 cubic cm

○ **C.** 1464 cubic cm

○ **D.** 2071 cubic cm

8   Including time for station stops, a train travels 475 miles in 11 hours, 15 minutes. Joel is considering driving his own car instead of taking the train, and wants to compare the time it would take to drive versus the time it would take to travel on the train. Joel figures he would be able to average about 50 miles per hour driving his own car.

Which of the following is the **best** estimate for the miles per hour rating that the train gets, with the stops included?

○ **A.** 28.8

○ **B.** 30

○ **C.** 40

○ **D.** 50

Go on ➤

9 The drawing of a tree trunk illustrates the basic shape of a cylinder. The trunk is cut at the point indicated.

Which of the following describes the resulting piece that is cut off?

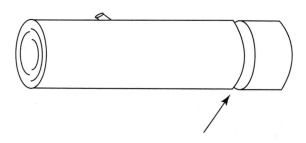

- ○ **A.** Sphere section

- ○ **B.** Cone section

- ○ **C.** Simple cylinder

- ○ **D.** Complex trapezoid section

10 A rectangular field has sides of 1,500 feet by 3,600 feet. A single fence connects two opposite corners of this field.

How long is the fence?

Explain in detail your answer using words, numbers, and/or diagrams.

```
┌──────────────────────────────────────────────────────────┐
│                                                            │
│                                                            │
│                                                            │
│                                                            │
│                                                            │
│                                                            │
│                                                            │
│                                                            │
│                                                            │
└──────────────────────────────────────────────────────────┘
```

Go on ➤

11   Which of the following describes a line that is not parallel to line R?

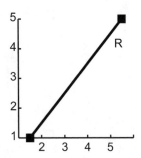

○ **A.** The line will have the same slope.

○ **B.** The line will be equidistant from line R.

○ **C.** The line will intersect line R only at the origin.

○ **D.** The line will intersect any other lines that are intersected by line R.

12   Which if the following best describes the figure below, in relation to the axis that is indicated?

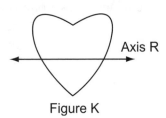

○ **A.** Figure K is not symmetrical, and the axis line demonstrates this.

○ **B.** Figure K is symmetrical, and the axis is drawn along a line of symmetry.

○ **C.** Figure K is symmetrical, but the axis line is not drawn along a line of symmetry.

○ **D.** Since Axis R bisects the figure at its linear center, Figure K is symmetrical since as much of the figure lies below the line as above it.

Go on ➤

13   A radio station runs a car giveaway promotion. For five days a key will be given out to the fifth caller when a particular song is played. After the five keys are awarded, one of those keys will be the correct one to start the car to determine the winner. You are one of the callers on a particular day, trying to win one of the keys.

Which of the following **best** describes the probabilities of winning the car?

○ **A.** Being awarded a key and then having the key that actually starts the car are dependent events.

○ **B.** Being awarded a key and then having the key that actually starts the car are independent events.

○ **C.** Since there are 5 callers and 5 keys awarded in two different events, the probability is 1 in 25 of winning the car.

○ **D.** Since there are 5 callers and 5 keys awarded in two different events, the probability is 1 in 125 of winning the car.

Go on ➤

14 Ana needs to roll a 6 in order to win the game. Ana has 3 chances to roll what she needs and is using a standard six-sided die.

What is the probability she'll get the roll she needs?

Explain in detail your work using words, numbers, and/or diagrams.

15　A school supply company test-marketed a new line of specimens for science teachers. The company has 12,800 science teachers on their catalog mailing list, and 1,000 of these teachers were selected at random to receive a shrink-wrapped rat specimen as a free example of the new product line. Only 28 teachers responded to this promotional mailing with orders. Another 31 teachers called to complain that sending a rat was somewhat offensive.

Which of the following conclusions can **best** be defended based on the information given?

○　**A.**　The sample of 1000 teachers was not representative of the company's customer base.

○　**B.**　The new line of specimens will not generate interest from the other 11,800 teachers on the main mailing list.

○　**C.**　The company should reasonably expect to receive about 280 new orders if they send this new product information to all of the teachers on their mailing list.

○　**D.**　The company should reasonably expect to receive about 330 new orders if they send this new product information to all of the teachers on their mailing list.

16　Which of the following coordinate points could be a solution for the line $2x + 3 = y$?

○　**A.**　(0, 4)

○　**B.**　(1, 5)

○　**C.**　(-1, 2)

○　**D.**　(3, 6)

Go on ➤

17 A pattern where the size of the members increases gradually is based on which of the following operations?

- ○ **A.** Addition
- ○ **B.** Subtraction
- ○ **C.** Division
- ○ **D.** Multiplication

Explain in detail your thinking using words, numbers, and/or diagrams.

The pattern in which members increase gradually is based on _____ .

Go on ➤

18   Which of the following is the correct equation for the line which passes through the points (4, -3) and (0, 0) ?

○ **A.** $2x - 3y = 0$

○ **B.** $3x + 4y = 0$

○ **C.** $3x - 4y = 0$

○ **D.** $-3/4 + y = x$

19   Line M is defined by which of the following equations?

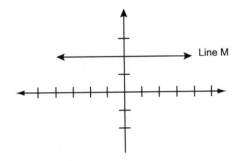

○ **A.** $1.5y = 3$

○ **B.** $2y = 2$

○ **C.** $y^2 = 1$

○ **D.** $y = 2x$

Go on ➤

20 Jill has $80,000 she plans to invest for four years. One investment is a partnership in a duplex apartment. This investment will yield no income in the first year, but would pay out a 12% return on the $80,000 invested in years 2, 3, and 4. The other investment is a limited partnership in a warehouse facility, which will pay out 6% in years 1 and 2, then 10% in years 3 and 4. Neither investment compounds the interest, but Jill will be able to withdraw her original $80,000 at the end of the four years if she chooses.

To the nearest dollar, how much more will she make if she goes with the apartment investment over the warehouse investment?

○ **A.** $3,200

○ **B.** $3,800

○ **C.** $4,800

○ **D.** $5,200

Go on ➤

21   A house had an original cost of $28,800 in 1962. When the house was sold in 1984, the sale price was $64,400. In 1992, the house was sold again, this time for $90,000. In 2001, the house was put on the market again, this time for an asking price of $140,000. It sold for $131,000. The owner of the house is planning to put the property up for sale in 2005, and plans to use the past pattern to assist in pricing the house.

What is the pattern for the increase in selling price for this property? Which of the previous sales is probably the **least** relevant to pricing the house this time?

Explain in detail your thinking using words, numbers, and/or diagrams to support your answer.

STOP

MATHEMATICS ASSESSMENT ONE—SESSION ONE SKILLS CHART

QUESTION	EALR. COMPONENT.GLE	ANSWER	KEYWORDS
1	NS01 1.1.1	B	Understand and apply scientific notation
2	NS06 1.1.4	C	Apply understanding of direct and inverse proportion
3	NS04 1.1.6	see analysis	Calculate using all forms of rational numbers
4	NS05 1.1.8	D	Apply estimation strategies to determine reasonableness of results
5	ME01 1.2.1	see analysis	Describe how changes in one or two dimensions affect area
6	ME02 1.2.3	B	Convert units of measure to achieve needed precision
7	ME03 1.2.5	B	Find the volume of a cylinder
8	ME04 1.2.6	C	Estimate reasonable measurement at appropriate precision
9	GS01 1.3.1	C	Understand characteristics of three-dimensional figures
10	GS01 1.3.2	see analysis	Apply understanding of geometric properties
11	GS02 1.3.3	C	Identify, interpret, and use the meaning of slope of a line
12	GS02 1.3.4	C	Examine figures to determine symmetry
13	PS01 1.4.1	A	Understand conditional probability
14	PS01 1.4.2	see analysis	Calculate probabilities
15	PS02 1.4.3	D	Apply appropriate methods to collect data
16	PS03 1.4.5	B	Determine whether the equation of a line is appropriate for data
17	AS01 1.5.1	A; see analysis	Apply processes that use repeated operations
18	AS01 1.5.2	B	Analyze a pattern to write an equation or rule
19	AS02 1.5.4	A	Apply understanding of equations to represent relationships
20	AS03 1.5.6	A	Apply procedures to solve equations
21	SR02 2.2.1	see analysis	Apply strategies to devise a plan to solve a problem

Mathematics Assessment One–Session One: Answer Key

1 Which of the following is the correct meaning for 4^5?
Analysis: Any number, when raised to a power, is equivalent to that number multiplied by itself the number of times indicated in the power. Therefore, 4^5 is equivalent to 4 multiplied by itself 5 times, or 4 x 4 x 4 x 4 x 4. *Choice B is correct.*

2 Which of the following would be the correct number to use to eliminate 7/3 from one side of an equation using multiplication as a tool for simplifying the equation?
Analysis: The correct number to use to eliminate 7/3 from one side of an equation using multiplication is the multiplicative inverse of that number, or 3/7: 7/3 x 3/7 = 1. *Choice C is correct.*

3 Simplify the expression $4^3 + 5$ x $7 - 16$. **Explain in detail** your work using words, numbers, and/or diagrams.
Analysis: The solution to this problem is 83, since $4^3 + 5$ x 7 - 16 = 64 + 5 x 7 - 16 = 64 + 35 - 16 = 83.

4 Jose likes to estimate grocery store purchases by rounding the prices of items put into the shopping cart to the nearest dollar, and keeping a mental tally of this total. Which of the following statements **best** describes Jose's estimation strategy in a practical sense?
Analysis: This kind of mental tally is an estimation strategy that produces reasonably close results, useful for the consumer in case a mistake has been made in computing the total grocery purchase. *Choice D is correct.*

5 A field that is rectangular in shape, measuring 200 feet wide by 600 feet long, will have its width increased by 50% before the next planting season. By what percent will the field's useable area increase? **Explain in detail** your work using words, numbers, and/or diagrams.
Analysis: Since the width of the field increases from 200 to 300 feet, the field's area will increase from 120,000 square feet to 180,000 square feet: 200 feet x 600 feet = 120,000 square feet, and 300 feet x 600 feet = 180,000 square feet. This is an increase of 60,000 sq. ft. or 50%.

6 Rhonda has been making a wooden deck for her house and has been cutting the pieces of wood by measuring to the nearest 1/8 of an inch. She's finding that some of the boards are ending up too long, while others are ending up too short, creating waste in materials and lost time. Which of the following steps would **most** likely solve her problem?
Analysis: If she's already working to 1/8 of an inch precision and it's not producing the results needed, tightening the precision to 1/16 of an inch makes the most sense. All of the other choices would lead to lessened precision. *Choice B is correct.*

7 Using the formula $V = \pi r^2 h$, determine the volume of a cylinder with a height of 12 cm and a radius of 6 cm to the nearest whole number. Use 3.1415 as a value for π.
Analysis: Using the formula $V = \pi r^2 h$ yields 1357.128 cubic cm: V = 3.1415 x 6^2 x 12 = 3.1415 x 36 x 12 = 1357.128. *Choice B is correct.*

8 Including time for station stops, a train travels 475 miles in 11 hours, 15 minutes. Joel is considering driving his own car instead of taking the train, and wants to compare the time it would take to drive versus the time it would take to travel on the train. Joel figures he would be able to average about 50 miles per hour driving his own car. Which of the following is the **best** estimate for the miles per hour rating that the train gets, with the stops included?
Analysis: The train seems to average about 40 mph on its trip (actual is 42.22) First convert the 15 minutes to a fraction of an hour (15 minutes = 0.25 hours) and divide the total miles by the number of hours to get the miles per hour rating for the train with the stops included: 475 ÷ 11.25 = 42.22. This is about 40 miles per hour. *Choice C is correct.*

9 The drawing of a tree trunk illustrates the basic shape of a cylinder. The trunk is cut at the point indicated. Which of the following describes the resulting piece that is cut off?

Analysis: A tree trunk is generally the basic shape of a cylinder. Therefore, the piece that would be cut off is just a portion of a longer cylinder. *Choice C is correct.*

MATHEMATICS ASSESSMENT ONE—SESSION ONE: ANSWER KEY

10 A rectangular field has sides of 1,500 feet by 3,600 feet. A single fence connects two opposite corners of this field. How long is that fence? **Explain in detail** your work using words, numbers, and/or diagrams.

Analysis: If a single fence were built to connect two opposite corners of this field, the length of fence needed could be looked at as the length of the hypotenuse of a right triangle. This problem can be solved using the Pythagorean Theorem, $a^2 + b^2 = c^2$: $1,500^2 + 3,600^2 = c^2$, $2,250,000 + 12,960,000 = 15,210,000$. The square root of $15,210,000$ is $3,900$ feet or $c = 3,900$ feet. Another way to solve this would be to recognize this as multiples of a 5-12-13 right triangle.

11 Which of the following describes a line that is not parallel to line R?

Analysis: Parallel lines do not intersect and they have the same slope. Also, a line that is parallel to line R will intersect any line that intersects line R. The only statement that is true of a line that is not parallel to R is that the line will intersect line R at the origin. *Choice C is correct.*

12 Which if the following best describes the figure below, in relation to the axis that is indicated?

Axis R

Figure K

Analysis: Figure K is symmetrical, but the axis line is not drawn along a line of symmetry. *Choice C is correct.*

13 A radio station runs a car giveaway promotion. For five days a key will be given out to the fifth caller when a particular song is played. After the five keys are awarded, one of those keys will be the correct one to start the car to determine the winner. You are one of the callers on a particular day, trying to win one of the keys. Which of the following **best** describes the probabilities of winning the car?

Analysis: Being awarded a key and then having the key that actually starts the car are dependent events. Having the chance to be one of five people to win the car first depends on being the fifth caller on a particular day. There is no way to determine any actual probabilities based on the information supplied in the problem. *Choice A is correct.*

14 Ana needs to roll a 6 in order to win the game. Ana has 3 chances to roll what she needs and is using a standard six-sided die. What is the probability she'll get the roll she needs? **Explain in detail** your work using words, numbers, and/or diagrams.

Analysis: The probability she'll get the roll she needs in one roll is 1/6. Because she has 3 chances to roll what she needs, the probability becomes 1/6 x 3 or 3/6. This is equivalent to a probability of 1/2.

15 A school supply company test-marketed a new line of specimens for science teachers. The company has 12,800 science teachers on their catalog mailing list, and 1,000 of these teachers were selected at random to receive a shrink-wrapped rat specimen as a free example of the new product line. Only 28 teachers responded to this promotional mailing with orders. Another 31 teachers called to complain that sending a rat was somewhat offensive. Which of the following conclusions can best be defended based on the information given?

Analysis: While the rat may be a poor choice to send as a promotional item, 28 orders were generated per 1,000 mailings. With 11,800 teachers on the list still to be contacted, new orders ought to correspond to those generated in the sample. That's about 28 per 1000, or 11.8 x 28 = 330.4 orders. *Choice D is correct.*

16 Which of the following coordinate points could be a solution for the line $2x + 3 = y$?

Analysis: Check the x value for each coordinate point in the equation to see if the equation yields the correct y value: $2(0) + 3 = 3$, not 4: $2(-1) + 3 = 1$, not 2; $2(3) + 3 = 9$, not 6, so the points in choices A, C, and D cannot be solutions for the line $2x + 3 = y$. However, $2(1) + 3 = 5$, so the point (1, 5) can be a solution of the line. *Choice B is correct.*

17 A pattern where the size of the members increases gradually is based on which of the following operations? **Explain in detail** your thinking using words, numbers, and/or diagrams.

Analysis: Multiplication patterns tend to increase rapidly, and subtraction/division patterns decline, so a pattern where the size of the members increases gradually is based on addition. *Choice A is correct.*

MATHEMATICS ASSESSMENT ONE—SESSION ONE: ANSWER KEY

18 Which of the following is the correct equation for the line which passes through the points (4, -3) and (0, 0)?
Analysis: The equation for the line which passes through the points (4, -3) and (0, 0) is $3x + 4y = 0$. This can be confirmed by substituting the coordinate values into the equation: $12 - 12 = 0$, and $0 + 0 = 0$. *Choice B is correct.*

19 Line M is defined by which of the following equations?

Analysis: Line M is defined by the equation $1.5y = 3$, since $1.5\ y = 3$ simplifies to $y = 2$. *Choice A is correct.*

20 Jill has $80,000 she plans to invest for four years. One investment is a partnership in a duplex apartment. This investment will yield no income in the first year, but would pay out a 12% return on the $80,000 invested in years 2, 3, and 4. The other investment is a limited partnership in a warehouse facility, which will pay out 6% in years 1 and 2, then 10% in years 3 and 4. Neither investment compounds the interest, but Jill will be able to withdraw her original $80,000 at the end of the four years if she chooses. To the nearest dollar, how much more will she make if she goes with the apartment investment over the warehouse investment?
Analysis: The apartment will pay $9,600 in years 2, 3, and 4, for a total of $28,800. The warehouse pays $4,800 in years 1 and 2, plus $8,000 in years 3 and 4, a total of $25,600. Therefore, she will make $3,200 more if she goes with the apartment over the warehouse: $28,800 - $25,600 = $3,200. *Choice A is correct.*

21 A house had an original cost of $28,800 in 1962. When the house was sold in 1984, the sale price was $64,400. In 1992, the house was sold again, this time for $90,000. In 2001, the house was put on the market for an asking price of $140,000. It sold for $131,000. The owner of the house is planning to put the property up for sale in 2005, and plans to use the past pattern to assist in pricing the house. What is the pattern for the increase in the selling price for this property? Which of the previous sales is probably the least relevant to pricing the house this time? **Explain in detail** your thinking using words, numbers, and/or diagrams.
Analysis: This pattern seems to roughly indicate a rise of about 50% in price per decade. That pattern is well established between the 1984 and 2001 sales, making 1962 the least relevant in the pattern.

MATHEMATICS ASSESSMENT ONE–SESSION TWO

On this part of the test you are **not** permitted to use tools such as a calculator, rulers, and manipulatives.

Turn to page 69 to read the Directions for Session Two of this Assessment. Then turn back to this page to begin.

22 The piece of construction paper shown is cut in the manner indicated and one piece is used for making an open-ended cylinder.

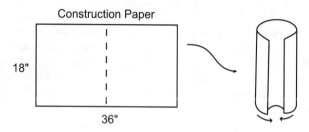

What will be the radius of this cylinder?

Explain in detail your work using words, numbers, and/or diagrams.

The radius of this cylinder is_____

Go on ➤

23   Which of the following equations would fit this set of data?

(-1, -5), (0, -1), (1, 3)

   ○ **A.** $y - 1 = x$

   ○ **B.** $4/5x - 4 = y$

   ○ **C.** $2x + 2 = y$

   ○ **D.** $y = 4x - 1$

24   Madeline has been shopping for space for her new office. The offices are priced according to the cost per year per square foot for the leased space. She has looked at suitable offices priced at $14.00, $16.00, $19.75, $14.00, and $26.00 per square foot.

Which measure of central tendency would probably give her the best idea of what to expect to pay for the lease?

   ○ **A.** Median

   ○ **B.** Quartile

   ○ **C.** Mode

   ○ **D.** Mean

Go on ➤

25   What is the value of y when x is 4 in the equation: $y = x^4$?

Explain in detail your work using words, numbers, and/or diagrams.

The value of y is _____ in this equation.

Go on ➤

26 Chuck wants to determine how many miles per gallon of gas his car is getting. At the station he filled the tank and noted the car's mileage (35,700) and how much he had paid per gallon ($1.98), as well as the total purchase amount of $25.00. After several days of driving he returned to the station and filled the tank again, noting that the mileage was now 35,900 and that it took 8 gallons of gas to refill the tank. The price paid per gallon on the second fill-up was $2.05, and the total purchase amount was $16.40.

How many miles was Chuck able to drive his car per gallon of gas?

○ **A.** 25

○ **B.** 22.5

○ **C.** 200

○ **D.** 8.60

Go on ➤

27 Kevin noticed that on game day a lot of people are looking for parking spaces. His front yard, if divided into parking spaces for compact cars only, could hold 8.8 cars. Allowing SUVs to park drops that figure to 7.2. The yard would hold 3.8 RVs, which could probably be charged $18.00 each for parking. Kevin thinks that people driving compact cars would pay $8.25 for a space, while he could get $9.75 for parking SUVs.

Parking what type of vehicle or combination of vehicle types would enable Kevin to make the greatest profit?

Explain in detail your thinking using words, numbers, and/or diagrams.

Go on ➤

28   Jill is slicing a 1.5-lb block of cheddar cheese into six slices as shown below.

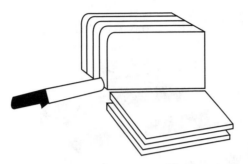

Estimate the weight of each slice of cheese if all of the slices are about equal.

Explain in detail your work using words, numbers, and/or diagrams.

The estimated weight of each slice of cheese is _____.

Go on ➤

29 Gill cut strips of a dark wood and strips of a light wood as part of a carpentry project. He glued them into a block. A section of wood was cut off the end as shown.

Which of the following would look like the cross-section?

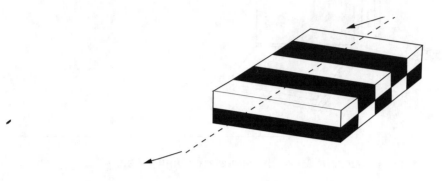

○ **A.**

○ **B.**

○ **C.**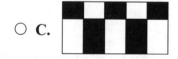

○ **D.**

Go on ➤

30   The table below shows sales for Andrew's Comic Book and Card Emporium, which opened on October 1.

Oct. $119.08	Nov. $245.55	Dec. $423.55	Jan. $112.07	Feb. $444.55
March $564.88	April $622.22	May $814.43	June $1200.94	July $298.84

Andrew, the store owner, has applied for a bank loan to buy additional inventory for his comic book business. While he is currently not selling enough merchandise to pay rent and utilities, Andrew believes the store is becoming better known, and that sales will improve during the current summer season.

Using the information in the table, explain why the bank would likely deny Andrew's loan.

Go on ➤

31 Edgar, doing research at his college for the registrar's office, found that over the last ten years only 28% of students who entered the college on a football scholarship had graduated. Interestingly, the school's head football coach was recently quoted as saying "80% of students who are on a football scholarship will graduate."

Which of the following **best** explains the disparity in what the two are saying about graduation rates for football scholarship students?

○ **A.** Edgar probably dislikes the football program, and his research must be biased.

○ **B.** The head football coach is lying in order to make his program look better.

○ **C.** Edgar's research covered past graduation rates, while the coach appears to be predicting future graduation rates.

○ **D.** Both Edgar and the head football coach are trying to use statistics to prove something that is subjective and cannot be proven.

32 Three houses sold in the River Bend subdivision in a single year. House 1 sold for $249,200 in January, House 2 sold for $239,900 in August, and House 3 sold for $272,800 in November.

Which of the following, based only on the data, can be said with the **most** certainty?

○ **A.** House 3 was the best house of the group.

○ **B.** House prices in this subdivision are steadily increasing.

○ **C.** The median house price in this subdivision is representative of the group.

○ **D.** The small amount of data makes developing or justifying a conclusion unsupportable.

Go on ➤

33 Which of the following situations represents the **best** opportunity to collect data that is not biased?

○ **A.** Polling bar owners about the fairness of a new tax to be collected on alcohol sales

○ **B.** Surveying sports fans about the feasibility of building a new stadium

○ **C.** Polling farmers about whether the rising cost of diesel fuel has been caused by oil companies

○ **D.** Surveying shoppers at a shopping mall about an upcoming school board election

Explain in detail your thinking using words, numbers, and/or diagrams.

Go on ➤

34 Which of the following would least affect the growth of a healthy fish population in a particular lake?

○ **A.** Amount of food available to the fish population

○ **B.** Removing a sampling of fish for a scientific study

○ **C.** Doubling the amount of fish that can be taken during fishing season

○ **D.** Draining part of the lake to build a new dock and boat ramp facility

Explain in detail your thinking using words, numbers, and/or diagrams.

Go on ➤

35 Domenica has collected the names and dates of birth for 100 people as part of an astrology research project.

What type of graphic representation would be the **best** way to organize this data?

Explain in detail your thinking using words, numbers, and/or diagrams.

36 Point C is located at (2, -2).

What would be its new coordinates if Point C is shifted down one unit and to the left 4 units?

○ **A.** (-2, -3)

○ **B.** (-3, -3)

○ **C.** (-2, 3)

○ **D.** (-3, 2)

Go on ➤

37   What is the slope for the equation $2x + 3y = 6$?

Explain in detail your work using words, numbers, and/or diagrams.

The slope for the equation is _____.

---

38   Simplify $\dfrac{2}{3}(7^2 - 1) + 12 \div \dfrac{1}{8}$.

○ **A.** 72

○ **B.** 96

○ **C.** 128

○ **D.** 142

Go on ➤

39 Walter is building a wooden storage building in his back yard. He thinks materials will cost from $1,425.00 up to $1,675.00, depending on waste and possible "unknowns." A neighbor's college-age son will help with the building for a flat rate of $18.75 an hour. Walter thinks he'll need about 15 hours of help, but perhaps as much as 20 hours depending on how things go.

What is the **least** amount this shed could cost once it is finished?

- ○ **A.** $280.25
- ○ **B.** $1,706.25
- ○ **C.** $2,050.00
- ○ **D.** $2,125.25

40 A rectangular prism has sides no less than 1 inch. The volume of this prism is 240 cubic inches, and the length is 20 inches.

Which of the following could be the width?

- ○ **A.** 0.5 inches
- ○ **B.** 3 inches
- ○ **C.** 12.5 inches
- ○ **D.** 14 inches

Go on ➤

41   In the equation, $2y - 4x = 4$, what is the value of y alone in terms of the rest of the equation?

   ○ **A.** $y = 2x + 2$

   ○ **B.** $y = 2x - 2$

   ○ **C.** $y = -2x + 4$

   ○ **D.** $y = 2x - 4$

42   Rhonda is going to use a cardboard box as a sign for her yard sale, writing on 4 sides of it so that it can be seen from any direction. She has a box that is essentially a cube, with sides of 18 inches. She sits this box on its base, then extends the flaps, which go 9 inches past the top of the box.

How much **more** surface area will extending the flaps on the top of the box give her for her sign?

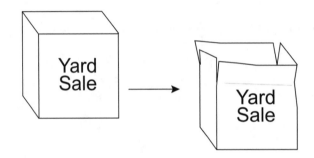

   ○ **A.** 2268 square inches

   ○ **B.** 1944 square inches

   ○ **C.** 648 square inches

   ○ **D.** 162 square inches

STOP

MATHEMATICS ASSESSMENT ONE—SESSION TWO SKILLS CHART

QUESTION	EALR. COMPONENT.GLE	ANSWER	KEYWORDS
22	CU02 4.2.2	see analysis	Express ideas and situations using mathematical language and notation
23	PS03 1.4.5	D	Analyze a linear model to judge appropriateness for a data set
24	PS03 1.4.6	A	Apply understanding of statistics to analyze data
25	AS03 1.5.5	see analysis	Apply procedures to simplify expressions
26	AS03 1.5.6	A	Apply procedures to solve equations
27	SR02 2.2.2	see analysis	Apply mathematical tools to solve problems
28	SR03 3.1.1	see analysis	Use two-dimensional and three-dimensional figures to solve problems
29	MC01 5.1.2	D	Understand how to use different models in the same situation
30	SR04 3.2.2	see analysis	Analyze information to draw conclusions
31	PS03 1.4.6	C	Analyze procedures to determine appropriateness of claims
32	SR05 3.3.3	C	Analyze thinking and mathematical ideas
33	CU01 4.1.1	D; see analysis	Understand how to collect mathematical information
34	CU01 4.1.2	B; see analysis	Synthesize mathematical information
35	CU02 4.2.1	see analysis	Analyze mathematical information to organize an argument
36	MC01 5.1.1	A	Determine coordinates of a point after transformations
37	MC01 5.1.2	see analysis	Find the equation of a line
38	NS04 1.1.6	C	Apply strategies to compute with rational numbers
39	NS05 1.1.8	B	Apply estimation strategies
40	ME01 1.2.1	B	Analyze the effect of changes to one or two dimensions of an object
41	AS03 1.5.6	A	Apply procedures to solve equations
42	GS01 1.3.2	C	Apply understanding of geometric properties

MATHEMATICS ASSESSMENT ONE—SESSION TWO: ANSWER KEY

22 The piece of construction paper shown is cut in the manner indicated and one piece is used for making an open-ended cylinder.

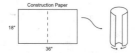

What will be the radius of this cylinder? **Explain in detail** your work using words, numbers, and/or diagrams.
Analysis: Recognizing that the newly created cylinder will have both a height and circumference of 18 inches, $C = \pi D$. Plugging in the known information, $18/3.1415 = D$, or $5.729 = D$. The radius is half of the diameter, so the radius is 2.86 inches.

23 Which of the following equations would fit this set of data?

(-1, -5), (0, -1), (1, 3)

Analysis: Substituting the values actually yields an exact match in this case. Using (1, 3) is a good data point for doing a quick check of the equations before narrowing the choices; $3 = 4 \times 1 - 1$; $3 = 4 - 1$; $3 = 3$ *Choice D is correct.*

24 Madeline has been shopping for space for her new office. The offices are priced according to the cost per year per square foot for the leased space. She has looked at suitable offices priced at $14.00, $16.00, $19.75, $14.00, and $26.00. Which measure of central tendency would probably give her the best idea of what to expect to pay for the lease?
Analysis: In this case the median looks most reliable for budgeting since there is a good supply of offices for less money, and no pressing need to pay $19-26 since the problem stated that all of the offices were suitable. *Choice A is correct.*

25 What is the value of y when x is 4 in the equation: $y = x^4$? **Explain in detail** your work using words, numbers, and/or diagrams.
Analysis: The value of y when x is 4 in the equation $y = x^4$ is 256, since $4^4 = 4 \times 4 \times 4 \times 4 = 256$.

26 Chuck wants to determine how many miles per gallon of gas his car is getting. At the station he filled the tank and noted the car's mileage (35,700) and how much he had paid per gallon ($1.98), as well as the total purchase amount of $25.00. After several days of driving he returned to the station and filled the tank again, noting that the mileage was now 35,900 and that it took 8 gallons of gas to refill the tank. The price paid per gallon on the second fill-up was $2.05, and the total purchase amount was $16.40. How many miles was Chuck able to drive his car per gallon of gas?
Analysis: In this problem there is a good deal of extra information. All that is needed to solve this problem is the number of miles traveled and the number of gallons of gas used to travel those miles. First, find the number of miles traveled by subtracting the initial number of miles on the car from the miles on the car at the second fill-up: 35,900 miles – 35,700 miles = 200 miles. Since the gas tank was full after the first fill-up, the number of gallons used is simply the number of gallons of gas required to fill the tank the second time, or 8 gallons. The answer is found by dividing the miles traveled by the the number of gallons used to travel that distance: 200 miles ÷ 8 gallons = 25 miles/gallon. *Choice A is correct.*

27 Kevin noticed that on game day a lot of people are looking for parking spaces. His front yard, if divided into parking spaces for compact cars only, could hold 8.8 cars. Allowing SUVs to park drops that figure to 7.2. The yard would hold 3.8 RVs, which could probably be charged $18.00 each for parking. Kevin thinks that people driving compact cars would pay $8.25 for a space, while he could get $9.75 for parking SUVs. Parking what type of vehicle or combination of vehicle types would enable Kevin to make the greatest profit? **Explain in detail** your thinking using words, numbers, and/or diagrams.
Analysis: This problem requires understanding that the yard is irregular and Kevin's measurements don't lead to whole number parking spaces. He'll only get paid for parking whole cars. If he parks compact cars only, he could make $8.25 x 8 = $66.00. Parking only SUVs, Kevin can make $9.75 x 7, or $68.25, and if he parked only RVs he would make $18.00 x 3, or $54.00. Parking a mixture of compact cars and SUVs would bring less profit than parking only SUVs. Kevin will make the greatest profit if he parks only SUVs.

28 Jill is slicing a 1.5-lb block of cheddar cheese into six slices as shown below.

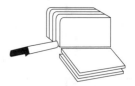

Estimate the weight of each slice of cheese if all of the slices are about equal. **Explain in detail** your work using words, numbers, and/or diagrams.
Analysis: A 1.5-pound block of cheese is 24 ounces (16 ounces per pound x 1.5 pounds = 24 ounces). It is cut into 6 slices. Therefore, the weight of each slice would be 24 ÷ 6 = 4 ounces.

MATHEMATICS ASSESSMENT ONE–SESSION TWO: ANSWER KEY

29 Gill cut strips of a dark wood and strips of a light wood as part of a carpentry project. He glued them into a block. A section of wood was cut off the end as shown.

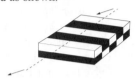

Which of the following would look like the cross-section?

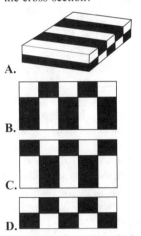

A.

B.

C.

D.

Analysis: Even though the line does cut through the figure at an angle, creating kind of a ramp from the side view, the cross section, viewed from straight on, would still look the same as the original figure viewed on end. *Choice D is correct.*

30 The table below shows sales for Andrew's Comic Book and Card Emporium, which opened on October 1.

Oct.	Nov.	Dec.	Jan.	Feb.
$119.08	$245.55	$423.55	$112.07	$444.55

March	April	May	June	July
$564.88	$622.22	$814.43	$1200.94	$298.84

Andrew, the store owner, has applied for a bank loan to buy additional inventory for his comic book business. While he is currently not selling enough merchandise to pay rent and utilities, Andrew believes the store is becoming better known, and that sales will improve during the current summer season. Using the information in the table, explain why the bank would likely deny Andrew's loan.

Analysis: Studying the data, it's not a particular month that can be blamed as the problem. Inconsistency in sales would even be okay if there were at least some months where sales figures were very high. The problem with Andrew's shop is that it has been in business nearly a year, and sales are not growing.

31 Edgar, doing research at his college for the registrar's office, found that over the last ten years only 28% of students who enter the college on a football scholarship had graduated. Interestingly, the school's head football coach was recently quoted as saying "80% of students who are on a football scholarship will graduate." Which of the following **best** explains the disparity in what the two are saying about graduation rates for football scholarship students?

Analysis: Edgar's research covered past graduation rates, while the coach appears to be predicting future graduation rates. The way this data can most easily be reconciled is to accept it as overlapping. The data about past graduation rates is fixed. Students who are still in the program and have not yet graduated would still have the opportunity to meet the 80% rate the coach is predicting. *Choice C is correct.*

32 Three houses sold in the River Bend subdivision in a single year. House 1 sold for $249,200 in January, House 2 sold for $239,900 in August, and House 3 sold for $272,800 in November. Which of the following, based only on the data, can be said with the most certainty?

Analysis: The median house price in this subdivision is representative of the group. While it is only a small data set, the premise of the question asks what can be said with the most certainty based on the data. The median house price is within 10% of the others, and it does appear to be representative of the group. *Choice C is correct.*

33 Which of the following situations represents the **best** opportunity to collect data that is not biased? **Explain in detail** your thinking using words, numbers, and/or diagrams.

Analysis: Surveying shoppers at a shopping mall about an upcoming school board election would probably represent the best opportunity to collect data that is not biased, since it provides a sample that is not as directly affected by the survey issue. *Choice D is correct.*

34 Which of the following would least affect the growth of a healthy fish population in a particular lake? **Explain in detail** your thinking using words, numbers, and/or diagrams.

Analysis: Since populations tend to naturally grow at an exponential rate, factors that can most affect the numbers of existing fish would tend to affect the population the most. Loss of food, loss of habitat, or increased pressure from predation would tend to affect the fish population much more than a sample removed for a study. *Choice B is correct.*

MATHEMATICS ASSESSMENT ONE—SESSION TWO: ANSWER KEY

35 Domenica has collected the names and dates of birth for 100 people as part of an astrology research project. What type of graphic representation would be the best way to organize this data? **Explain in detail** your thinking using words, numbers, and/or diagrams.
Analysis: A table would probably be the best way to organize this data, since this kind of data is ideally suited to tables and spreadsheets.

36 Point C is located at (2, -2). What would be its new coordinates if Point C is shifted down one unit and to the left 4 units?
Analysis: Shifting point C a single unit down moves it to the coordinates (2, -3), and then shifting it 4 units to the left brings point C to (-2,- 3). *Choice A is correct.*

37 What is the slope for the equation $2x + 3y = 6$? **Explain in detail** your work using words, numbers, and/or diagrams.
Analysis: This can be solved by using $y = mx + b$ and then solving for y. $3y = -2x + 6$, and then $y = -2/3x + 2$. The slope of this line is -2/3.

38 Simplify $2/3 (7^2 - 1) + 12 \div 1/8$.
Analysis: This simplifies to $2/3(48) + (12 \times 8/1) = 32 + 96 = 128$. *Choice C is correct.*

39 Walter is building a wooden storage building in his back yard. He thinks materials will cost from $1,425.00 up to $1,675.00, depending on waste and possible "unknowns." A neighbor's college-age son will help with the building for a flat rate of $18.75 an hour. Walter thinks he'll need about 15 hours of help, but perhaps as much as 20 hours depending on how things go. What is the least amount this shed could cost once it is finished?
Analysis: The least amount this shed could cost once it is finished can be found by taking the low-end estimate for materials and adding the low-end estimate for the labor: $1,425 + (15 \times $18.75) = $1,706.25. *Choice B is correct.*

40 A rectangular prism has sides no less than 1 inch. The volume of this prism is 240 cubic inches, and the length is 20 inches. Which of the following could be the width?
Analysis: At first it looks like something may be missing from this problem, but using the formula for volume, $V = h \times w \times h$, you find that $h \times w \times 20 = 240$. If 240 is divided by 20, the result must be the product of both height and width. Since 240 cubic inches $\div$ 20 inches = 12 inches, then $h \times w$ must equal 12 inches, with neither being less than 1. Choice A is less than one and the rest of the choices are greater than 12 inches except choice B, 3 inches. Of the choices, the only result that could be the width is 3 inches. *Choice B is correct.*

41 In the equation $2y - 4x = 4$, what is the value of y alone in terms of the rest of the equation?
Analysis: The equation $2y - 4x = 4$ is equivalent to $2y = 4x + 4$. Once the equation is stated in terms of y, factor out a 2 from the equation to place it in lowest terms: $2y = 4x + 4$ is equivalent to $y = 2x + 2$. *Choice A is correct.*

42 Rhonda is going to use a cardboard box as a sign for her yard sale, writing on 4 sides of it so that it can be seen from any direction. She has a box that is essentially a cube, with sides of 18 inches. She sits this box on its base, then extends the flaps, which go 9 inches past the top of the box. How much **more** surface area will extending the flaps on the top of the box give her for her sign?

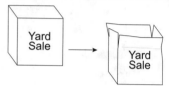

Analysis: The question asks how much surface area will be added for the sign by extending the flaps on the top of the box. With the flaps extended, the sign will have 4 sides with an added height of 9 inches and a width of 18 inches. To solve this problem, find the area that extending the flaps will add to the sign. First find the area of one of the flaps and multiply that area by the 4 sides: $4(18 \times 9) = 4 \times 162 = 648$ square inches. *Choice C is correct.*

MATHEMATICS ASSESSMENT TWO—SESSION ONE

On this part of the test you are permitted to use tools such as a calculator, rulers, and manipulatives.

Turn to page 69 to read the Directions for Session One of this Assessment. Then turn back to this page to begin.

1   Express 544,000,000 using scientific notation.

Explain in detail your work using words, numbers, and/or diagrams.

2   A scientist caught, tagged, and released back into a lake 75 trout. At the end of the next 30 days the scientist caught 100 trout, 5 of which were tagged from the previous catch and release.

Which of the following would be the **best** estimate of the total trout population in this lake based only on the results of the research?

○ **A.** 750

○ **B.** 1,500

○ **C.** 7,500

○ **D.** 12,750

Go on ➤

3 Simplify $4(5^2 + 5^2) - 25$.

    ○ **A.** 75

    ○ **B.** 125

    ○ **C.** 175

    ○ **D.** 225

4 The surface area of a rectangular coffee table is 840 square inches. The width is changed from 20 inches to 24 inches, but the length remains the same.

What will be the new surface area of the coffee table?

Explain in detail your work using words, numbers, and/or diagrams.

The surface area of the new coffee table will be_____.

Go on ➤

5   Ernest has produced 9 gallons of homemade cider. He plans to sell 3 gallons of this cider to pay for the cost of making it, then split the rest equally among himself and three friends who helped pick the apples.

How much cider will each friend receive?

○ **A.** 2.5 quarts

○ **B.** 3.5 quarts

○ **C.** 5 quarts

○ **D.** 6 quarts

6   If you use 3.1415 as a value for π, and you also know the height of a particular cylinder, then which of the following statements is true?

○ **A.** The surface area of the cylinder may be determined.

○ **B.** The volume of the cylinder may be determined.

○ **C.** The radius of the cylinder may be determined by using either the volume formula or the surface area formula.

○ **D.** Not enough information is known about the cylinder to determine its surface area or volume.

7   Which of the following has only two sides that meet at greater than a ninety-degree angle?

○ **A.** Right triangle

○ **B.** Parallelogram

○ **C.** Rhombus

○ **D.** Regular octagon

Go on ➤

8 Corrine has made a mold to pour concrete in the form of a cylinder. She plans to make 4 cylinders that will become decorative legs for an outdoor bench. Each leg is to be 12 inches high, with a radius of 4 inches. She is thinking of increasing the mold height in order to make a leg that is 14 inches tall. For each inch of added height, about how many more cubic inches of concrete must be used?

Explain in detail your thinking using words, numbers, and/or diagrams.

About_____cubic inches of concrete must be used.

Go on ➤

9   Which of the following can be ruled out as a description of the triangle formed by points TSR?

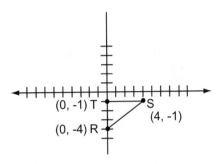

○ **A.** It is a right triangle.

○ **B.** TSR's points all have negative coordinates, so its area cannot be determined.

○ **C.** The Pythagorean theorem could be used for determining the length of side SR.

○ **D.** The sum of sides TS and TR is greater than the length of side SR, even though SR is longer than either side.

Go on ➤

10   Ms. Mills has one of 200 tickets sold for the school band raffle. In the raffle there are 3 prizes: a grand prize, a first prize, and a second prize. Once a winning ticket is drawn, it is not replaced into the drawing.

The grand prize winner is drawn first, and Ms. Mills does not win. What is her chance of winning the first prize?

If she wins neither the grand prize nor the first prize, what is Ms. Mills' chance of winning the second prize?

Explain in detail your answer using words, numbers, and/or pictures.

Go on ➤

11   A weather person noted that in 14 of the last 20 years it rained on April 14. Going back 50 years, it had rained 38 times on the same date.

What is the mathematical probability that it will either rain or not rain on April 14 of this coming year?

○ **A.** 1 of 2

○ **B.** 14 of 20

○ **C.** 38 of 50

○ **D.** 52 of 70

12   Medical authorities reported that 12% of people in central Asia who contract the EBX34A virus survive it. The report was based on studies of five different EBX34A outbreaks involving some 8,500 people.

Which of the following **best** explains why, if an EBX34A outbreak were to happen in rural Canada, the same survival rate could not reasonably be assumed?

○ **A.** Too little data, since only five outbreaks were used for predicting the 12% survival rate

○ **B.** Incompatible samples, since the central Asia survivors represent a different population

○ **C.** Insufficient research, since the number of people who actually died of the EBX34A virus was not stated

○ **D.** Insufficient research, since the number of people who actually survived the EBX34A virus was not stated

Go on ➤

13   What is the key to the pattern below?

5600, 2800, 1400, 700, 350, 175

Explain in detail your thinking using words, numbers, and/or diagrams.

14   Which statement **best** describes the line below?

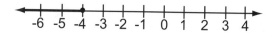

○ **A.** $y = -4$

○ **B.** $-y \leq -4$

○ **C.** $2y \geq -4$

○ **D.** $3y \leq -12$

Go on ➤

15   The hot dog stand charges $1.75 for a basic hot dog and $0.85 for a drink. The "special" includes a hot dog, a drink, and a bag of chips. The special costs only a nickel more than the hot dog and drink alone.

Which of the following is a simplified equation that would figure the total purchase amount regardless of the number of specials, S, purchased?

○ **A.** Total purchase = ($1.75)$S$ + ($ 0.85)

○ **B.** Total purchase = ($1.75)$S$ + ($ 0.85)S + ($ 0.05)

○ **C.** Total purchase = ($2.60)$S$

○ **D.** Total purchase = ($2.65)$S$

Go on ➤

16 Kasel's Suits and Tailoring has suits that cost $369.00 each plus a $12.00 tailoring fee that is added if the suit needs any adjustments. A customer's bill totaled $1,500.00.

What has he most likely purchased?

Explain in detail your thinking using words, numbers, and/or diagrams.

Go on ➤

17   In this value system of spheres, square pyramids, cubes, and cylinders, which shape has the highest value?

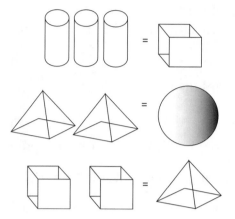

○ **A.** A sphere

○ **B.** A square pyramid

○ **C.** A cube

○ **D.** A cylinder

Go on ➤

18   A drug company recently published results of a study for a new drug to treat patients who suffer from softening of the teeth. Of those taking the new drug, 46% experienced hardening of their teeth. Part of this same study involved giving another group of patients a placebo, a harmless substance of no medicinal value. Of this second group of patients, 38% experienced the same teeth hardening. The drug company has characterized the new drug as "Quite promising, based on early testing and evaluation."

Which of the following conclusions **best** characterizes the results indicated by the data, not the company's comments?

○ **A.** The new drug is quite effective at hardening the teeth of patients with soft teeth problems.

○ **B.** The placebo is quite effective at hardening the teeth of patients with soft teeth problems.

○ **C.** The placebo, if used with the actual drug, would have an effective rate of 84%, making it clear that the two should be used together for the best result.

○ **D.** Patients taking the placebo had almost the same rate of teeth hardening as those taking the new drug, so the new drug may be mostly ineffective.

Explain in detail your thinking using words, numbers, and/or diagrams.

Go on ➤

19   A club has sold 2,249 tickets for a drawing. Tickets are to be drawn for small prizes, such as televisions and jewelry, with the ticket holders redeeming their ticket stubs for those prizes. The last drawing, the grand prize, will be for a new sports car.

How could the club **best** ensure that the drawing is fair for all ticket holders in terms of winning the grand prize?

Go on ➤

20 If a quick sketch is needed to show the line $2x - 4 = y$, which of the rough graphs would best demonstrate the data points on this line?

○ **A.**

○ **B.**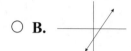

○ **C.**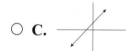

○ **D.**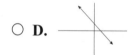

21 If you needed to solve the equation below in terms of x, which of the steps would make the most sense to perform first?

$4x = 34y$

○ **A.** Divide by y to eliminate it from the equation.

○ **B.** Divide each side by 2.

○ **C.** Divide each side by 4.

○ **D.** Subtract 2 from each side, leaving multiples which can be evenly divided in a later step.

STOP

MATHEMATICS ASSESSMENT TWO—SESSION ONE SKILLS CHART

QUESTION	EALR. COMPONENT.GLE	ANSWER	KEYWORDS
1	NS01 1.1.1	see analysis	Understand and apply scientific notation
2	NS02 1.1.4	B	Apply understanding of proportion to solve problems
3	NS04 1.1.6	C	Compute with rational numbers
4	ME01 1.2.1	see analysis	Analyze how changes in dimensions of an object affect area
5	ME02 1.2.3	D	Convert units of measure within systems
6	ME03 1.2.5	D	Apply formulas to calculate measurements of cylinders
7	GS01 1.3.1	D	Understand relationships among characteristics of figures
8	GS01 1.3.2	see analysis	Use properties of three-dimensional shapes to solve problems
9	GS02 1.3.3	B	Apply understanding of geometry properties
10	PS01 1.4.1	see analysis	Understand the concept of dependent events
11	PS01 1.4.2	A	Determine probabilities
12	PS02 1.4.3	B	Evaluate methods used to investigate a research question
13	AS01 1.5.1	see analysis	Recognize, extend, or create a pattern between sets of numbers
14	AS01 1.5.2	D	Find the equation of a line
15	AS02 1.5.4	D	Select an expression or equation to represent a real-world situation
16	SR02 2.2.2	see analysis	Apply mathematical tools to solve problems
17	SR04 3.2.1	A	Draw conclusions
18	SR05 3.3.3	D; see analysis	Examine data. Check for reasonableness of results
19	CU01 4.1.1	see analysis	Develop or apply an efficient system for collecting mathematical information
20	PS03 1.4.5	B	Match an equation with data
21	AS03 1.5.5	C	Apply procedures to simplify expressions

MATHEMATICS ASSESSMENT TWO–SESSION ONE: ANSWER KEY

1 Express 544,000,000 using scientific notation. **Explain in detail** your work using words, numbers, and/or diagrams.
Analysis: Using scientific notation, the coefficient is traditionally expressed as a number greater than 1 but less than 10, with the exponent portion expressed as a power of 10. Therefore, using scientific notation, 544,000,000 should be expressed as 5.44×10^8.

2 A scientist caught, tagged, and released back into a lake 75 trout. At the end of the next 30 days the scientist caught 100 trout, 5 of which were tagged from the previous catch and release. Which of the following would be the best estimate of the total trout population in this lake based only on the results of the research?
Analysis: Since 5% of the trout caught in the second phase of this experiment were tagged from the first, a reasonable estimate holds that 75 trout will represent 5% of the total trout population in the lake. Find the number of trout by multiplying the initial 75 trout by 20, or the number of times 75 will go into the 100% of the trout in the lake: 75 trout x 20 = 1,500 trout. *Choice B is correct.*

3 Simplify $4(5^2 + 5^2) - 25$.
Analysis: Since $4(5^2 + 5^2) - 25$ is equivalent to $4(25 + 25) - 25$, and $200 - 25 = 175$, the answer is 175. *Choice C is correct.*

4 The surface area of a rectangular coffee table is 840 square inches. The width is changed from 20 inches to 24 inches, but the length remains the same. What will be the new surface area of the coffee table? **Explain in detail** your work using words, numbers, and/or diagrams.
Analysis: In this problem, the first step is to get the length of the table. This can be found by dividing the surface area of the original table by its width: 840 square inches ÷ 20 inches = 42 inches. The new table will be 42 inches by 24 inches. Multiply the width of the new table by the length of the table to find the surface area of the new coffee table. 42 inches x 24 inches = 1008 square inches.

5 Ernest has produced 9 gallons of homemade cider. He plans to sell 3 gallons of this cider to pay for the cost of making it, then split the rest equally among himself and three friends who helped pick the apples. How much cider will each friend receive?
Analysis: After selling 3 of his 9 gallons of cider, Ernest has 6 gallons left to share. Since there are 4 quarts in a gallon, and Ernest has six gallons, he has 24 quarts to split 4 ways. Divide the 24 quarts by the 4 people the cider will be split amongst, and you find that each person will receive 6 quarts. *Choice D is correct.*

6 If you use 3.1415 as a value for π, and you also know the height of a particular cylinder, then which of the following statements is true?
Analysis: The parts of the formula for volume involve knowing two of the following three values: radius, height, and volume. The third may be determined if either of the other two are known; the same is true of the formula for surface area. There is not enough information provided in the question to determine either. *Choice D is correct.*

7 Which of the following has only two sides that meet at greater than a ninety-degree angle?
Analysis: The sides in a regular octagon will meet to form 135-degree angles. All of the other choices can have sides that meet at less than a ninety-degree angle. *Choice D is correct.*

8 Corrine has made a mold to pour concrete in the form of a cylinder. She plans to make 4 cylinders that will become decorative legs for an outdoor bench. Each leg is to be 12 inches high, with a radius of 4 inches. She is thinking of increasing the mold height in order to make a leg that is 14 inches tall. For each inch of added height, about how many more cubic inches of concrete must be used? **Explain in detail** your thinking using words, numbers, and/or diagrams to support your answer.
Analysis: Use the formula for the volume of a cylinder. In this case, though, the height will be 1: $V = 3.1415 (4^2)1 = 50.264$.

MATHEMATICS ASSESSMENT TWO–SESSION ONE: ANSWER KEY

9 Which of the following can be ruled out as a description of the triangle formed by points TSR?

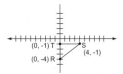

Analysis: This triangle's points (and its segments) aren't really negative; they simply define a coordinate location for this triangle. The lengths of TS and TR can be determined by inspection, and the area may easily be found. *Choice B is correct.*

10 Ms. Mills has one of 200 tickets sold for the school band raffle. In the raffle there are 3 prizes: a grand prize, a first prize, and a second prize. Once a winning ticket is drawn, it is not replaced into the drawing. The grand prize winner is drawn first, and Ms. Mills does not win. What is her chance of winning the first prize? If she wins neither the grand prize nor the first prize, what is Ms. Mills' chance of winning the second prize?
Analysis: Ms. Mills has one of 200 tickets in the drawing. Her chance of winning the grand prize is 1/200. Her chance of winning the first prize is 1/199. If she wins neither the grand prize nor the first prize, her chance of winning the second prize is 1/198.

11 A weather person noted that in 14 of the last 20 years it rained on April 14. Going back 50 years, it had rained 38 times on the same date. What is the mathematical probability that it will either rain or not rain on April 14 of this coming year?
Analysis: Data collected over time appears to point to the likelihood of a rainy day on April 14. However, in a mathematical sense, there are only two possible outcomes: it will either rain or it will not rain. There is a 1 in 2 chance of rain on April 14. *Choice A is correct.*

12 Medical authorities reported that 12% of people in central Asia who contract the EBX34A virus survive it. The report was based on studies of five different EBX34A outbreaks involving some 8,500 people. Which of the following **best** explains why, if an EBX34A outbreak were to happen in rural Canada, the same survival rate could not reasonably be assumed?
Analysis: As is often true in research, a sample from one population cannot automatically be adapted to predict what will happen in a different population. One might reasonably expect a disease would not spread as fast in rural Canada, better treatment may be available, etc., making a sample from one population incompatible with another population. *Choice B is correct.*

13 What is the key to the pattern below? **Explain in detail** your thinking using words, numbers, and/or diagrams.

5600, 2800, 1400, 700, 350, 175

Analysis: Each number is half of the previous number, so the key is to divide by 2 at each interval.

14 Which statement best describes the line below?

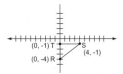

Analysis: Simplify the statements in choices C and D to lowest terms. In Choice C, $2y \geq -4$ may be simplified to $y \geq -2$. In Choice D, $3y \leq -12$ may be simplified to $y \leq -4$. *Choice D is correct.*

15 The hot dog stand charges $1.75 for a basic hot dog and $0.85 for a drink. The "special" includes a hot dog, a drink, and a bag of chips. The special costs only a nickel more than the hot dog and drink alone. Which of the following is a simplified equation that would figure the total purchase amount regardless of the number of specials, *S*, purchased?
Analysis: The special costs $2.65 each: $1.75 + $0.85 + $0.05 = $2.65. If *S* stands for any number of specials purchased, a simplified equation that would figure the total purchase amount regardless of the number of specials, *S*, purchased is total purchase = ($2.65)*S*. *Choice D is correct.*

16 Kasel's Suits and Tailoring has suits that cost $369.00 each plus a $12.00 tailoring fee that is added if the suit needs any adjustments. A customer's bill totaled $1,500.00. What has he most likely purchased? **Explain in detail** your thinking using words, numbers, and/or diagrams.
Analysis: A customer bought 4 suits and paid for two of them to be tailored. This problem could be set up and solved as a function of variables, which computes suits with tailoring and those without. It is probably easier to work backwards, taking an answer that looks close and figuring the true cost. In this case 4 suits cost 4 x $369 = $1,476.00. Next, subtract $1,476.00 from $1,500.00 and find that there was an additional $24.00 spent. That is the cost of tailoring for 2 suits ($12.00 x 2).

MATHEMATICS ASSESSMENT TWO—SESSION ONE: ANSWER KEY

17 In this value system of spheres, square pyramids, cubes, and cylinders, which shape has the highest value?

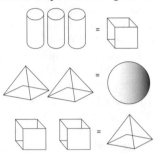

Analysis: A sphere is equal to 2 square pyramids. A square pyramid is more than a single cube, and a cube is much more than a cylinder. Therefore, the shape that has the highest value is the sphere. *Choice A is correct.*

18 A drug company recently published results of a study for a new drug to treat patients who suffered from softening of the teeth. Of those taking the new drug, 46% experienced hardening of their teeth. Part of this same study involved giving another group of patients a placebo, a harmless substance of no medicinal value. Of this second group of patients, 38% experienced the same teeth hardening. The drug company has characterized the new drug as "Quite promising, based on early testing and evaluation." Which of the following conclusions **best** characterizes the results indicated by the data, not the company's comments? **Explain in detail** your thinking using words, numbers, and/or diagrams.
Analysis: The new drug may be mostly ineffective since the new drug appears to be only mildly effective compared to people whose teeth got better with no medicine at all. *Choice D is correct.*

19 A club has sold 2,249 tickets for a drawing. Tickets are to be drawn for small prizes, such as televisions and jewelry, with the ticket holders redeeming their ticket stubs for those prizes. The last drawing, the grand prize, will be for a new sports car. How could the club **best** ensure that the drawing is fair for all ticket holders in terms of winning the grand prize?
Analysis: Replacing tickets back into the drawing for the car after the smaller prizes are won would best ensure that the drawing is fair for all ticket holders in terms of winning the grand prize. This gives each ticket holder an equivalent chance to win the car.

20 If a quick sketch is needed to show the line $2x - 4 = y$, which of the rough graphs would best demonstrate the data points on this line?
Analysis: The slope is positive, so the graph should point upward from left to right. *Choice B is correct.*

21 If you needed to solve the equation below in terms of x, which of the steps would make the most sense to perform first?
Analysis: In order to solve the equation below in terms of x it would make the most sense to first divide each side by 4, since division by 4 would yield $x = 34/4y$. *Choice C is correct.*

MATHEMATICS ASSESSMENT TWO—SESSION TWO

On this part of the test you are **not** permitted to use tools such as a calculator, rulers, and manipulatives.

Turn to page 69 to read the Directions for Session Two of this Assessment. Then turn back to this page to begin.

22   Karen is working on the labeling for a new kind of soft drink that her marketing company is helping to promote. The can will be 5.5 inches tall and have a radius of 1.75 inches.

About how much space is available on the sides of this can for labeling the product?

Explain in detail your work using words, numbers, and/or diagrams.

> **There is _____ of space available on the sides of this can.**

Go on ➤

23 On a multiple-choice test, Kate glanced at the problem below and decided that the answer must be "about 3"; therefore, any answers outside that range could be eliminated.

Using her strategy of estimation, which of the following could be ruled out as a reasonable answer for the problem?

$$2 \underline{} + \frac{1}{3} + \frac{1}{5} = \underline{}$$

○ **A.** $2\frac{7}{8}$

○ **B.** $\frac{56}{20}$

○ **C.** $3\frac{1}{8}$

○ **D.** $\frac{15}{12}$

24 A square measures 7 centimeters along a side.

How many lines of symmetry could be drawn through such a square?

○ **A.** 4

○ **B.** 6

○ **C.** 7

○ **D.** 8

Go on ➤

25   An art museum in New York gets about three million visitors per year.

About how many visitors should the museum be prepared to receive per week?

Explain in detail your answer using words, numbers, and/or diagrams.

The museum should have about____visitors per week.

Go on ➤

26 Jim started a new company 14 months ago recycling animal manure into useable fuels. Sales for his company have increased steadily since its founding. Jim has noticed that month-over-month sales appear to follow the pattern given below:

(previous month's sales) x 2 = next month's sales

The company's sales figures were plotted on a graph.

Which of the following would **best** describe this data?

○ **A.** The data is linear with no exceptions.

○ **B.** The data is basically linear, but with breaks in that line as new sales figures come in.

○ **C.** The data may appear to be linear in the first few months, but it would turn into a curve as the sales figures rapidly escalate.

○ **D.** The data is inconclusive about this company's sales, since the growth rate cannot be maintained at this level over a period of time.

27 Rainfall was 0.5 incheson Monday, 0.75 inches on Tuesday, and 1.00 inches on Wednesday. On Friday, rainfall was 1.5 inches. Brian was away on Thursday and unable to measure the rainfall on that day, but he put in his journal for Thursday, "It rained 1.25 inches today."

Which of the following **best** describes the accuracy of this entry?

○ **A.** It corresponds to the recorded rainfall trend and is likely correct.

○ **B.** It does not correspond to the recorded rainfall trend, and therefore cannot be correct.

○ **C.** It corresponds to the recorded rainfall trend, but since the data is not known, no reasonable conclusion can be drawn.

○ **D.** It can be confirmed as correct only with one more day of data in the set, since that would provide enough data set members to confirm the pattern.

Go on ➤

28   Which of the following is the simplified $y = mx + b$ version of the equation $4x - 4 = 8y$?

   ○ **A.** $y = \dfrac{1}{2}x - \dfrac{1}{2}$

   ○ **B.** $2y = x - \dfrac{1}{2}$

   ○ **C.** $y = 2x - 1$

   ○ **D.** $4y = x - \dfrac{1}{8}$

Go on ➤

29 On Monday, an oil company's stock rose from $108.00 to $110.16 on news that the company would receive special tax advantages. On Tuesday, the stock rose to $112.36 after being awarded a low-cost lease to drill on government lands. On Wednesday, the company announced that it would move some of its operations off-shore, thereby avoiding the payment of certain taxes; the stock closed up that day at $114.60. On Thursday, investors began buying the stock with renewed interest, and on that new volume it closed at $116.89. On Friday, it was announced that the government was exempting oil companies for responsibility in clean-ups related to chemical spills, and the stock again closed up, at $119.22. Over the weekend, it was announced by company representatives that they would no longer fund employee pension plans, thereby saving the company future expenses.

What should the stock close at on Monday, if the stock price reacts in the same way it has to previous news?

Explain in detail your thinking using words, numbers, and/or diagrams.

Go on >

30 Corrine plans to paint a living room and a bedroom the same color of paint. The paint costs $21.99 per gallon, and a single gallon is enough to cover 2,200 square feet. She plans to apply two coats of paint in both rooms. The living room is exactly 1.5 times the size of the bedroom. The paint may also be purchased by the quart, at a cost of $11.99. The instructions on the back of the can state that a quart will only cover 500 square feet, which is not 25% of what the gallon can states as the coverage for a full gallon of paint.

What information must still be known before a reasonable cost estimate for paint can be determined for this job?

○ **A.** The number of quarts versus gallons that will be bought for the job

○ **B.** The measurements of regions to be painted in both rooms

○ **C.** The measurements of regions to be painted in the bedroom only

○ **D.** The cost of other necessary supplies such as brushes and rollers

31 What is the cross-section of a three-dimensional figure?

○ **A.** A point or a line

○ **B.** A two-dimensional figure

○ **C.** Another three-dimensional figure

○ **D.** An identical three-dimensional figure

Go on ➤

32   A rectangular prism with a height of 12 cm, a width of 12 cm, and a length of 20 cm will have the height expanded to 16 cm.

About how much larger in percentage is the new figure?

Explain in detail your work using words, numbers, and/or diagrams.

Go on ➤

33 A sausage maker guarantees that not less than 62.2% of its pork sausage is made of pork. Based only on this information, which of the following would be impossible to support?

○ **A.** The sausage could have up to 37.8% beef in it.

○ **B.** The sausage must not have any grain or cereal filler in it.

○ **C.** The sausage could actually be up to 88.8 % pork.

○ **D.** The sausage could actually contain twice as much pork as non-pork ingredients.

Explain in detail your thinking using words, numbers, and/or diagrams.

Go on ➤

34   Owen works for a jewelry manufacturing company that specializes in making gold jewelry. Over the past five years, Owen has tracked the price of gold, his company's total sales, and his company's profits.

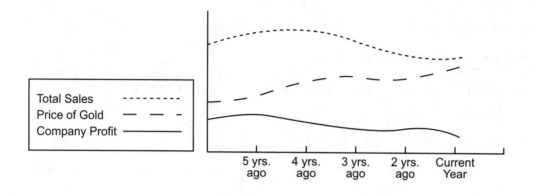

Which of the following statements has the least basis to be defended, based on the data shown?

○ **A.** Company profits appear to be gradually declining.

○ **B.** Rising gold prices tend to put pressure on profits.

○ **C.** Until about 2 years ago, there was a close correlation between sales and profits.

○ **D.** Profits will rise again once the price of gold has dropped to previous levels.

Explain in detail your thinking using words, numbers, and/or diagrams.

Go on ➤

35 Russell developed a table to describe the amount of money that is owed, depending on how many large pretzels a customer orders at his pretzel stand.

Number of Pretzels	Amount Owed
1	$0.89
2	$1.78
3	$2.57
4	$3.36
5	$4.05

Based on the information given, which of the following formulas would work for determining the purchase amount, A, regardless of the number of pretzels, P, ordered?

○ **A.** A = P(0.89)

○ **B.** A = P(0.89) + P(0.79)

○ **C.** A = P(0.89) + P(0.79) + P(0.69)

○ **D.** Since the cost for additional pretzels declines after the purchase of two, the pattern, if any, is not defined.

36 The point (1, 1) is an equidistant point for which of the following pairs of points?

○ **A.** (-1, -1) and (3, 3)

○ **B.** (1, 3) and (1, -2)

○ **C.** (3, 0) and (0, 1)

○ **D.** (-1, 1) and (1, 3)

Go on ➤

37   What is the slope of the line that passes through the points (1, 2) and (5, 2)?

Explain in detail your work using words, numbers, and/or diagrams.

38   Which of the following is the equivalent of 1,075 centimeters?

- ○ **A.** 1.075 meters

- ○ **B.** 10.75 meters

- ○ **C.** 107.5 meters

- ○ **D.** .1075 kilometers

Go on ➤

39 What is the volume of a cylinder that has a diameter of 10 inches and a height of 2.5 times that size?

○ **A.** 392.68 cubic inches

○ **B.** 1,024 cubic inches

○ **C.** 1,963.43 cubic inches

○ **D.** 7,853.75 cubic inches

40 Kylie knows the drive to her grandmother's house usually takes about 5 hours, 45 minutes. Her grandmother's house is 288 miles from Kylie's house, but they'll actually be starting their trip from her aunt's house, which adds another sixteen miles to their trip.

What kind of pace can Kylie expect on this trip if things go as they usually do?

○ **A.** About 40 mph

○ **B.** About 50 mph

○ **C.** About 60 mph

○ **D.** About 72 mph

Go on ➤

41   Every six or seven weeks, Karen's Turkey Farm is able to take 2,000 birds to market, each weighing about 8 pounds. The wholesale price of turkeys is usually in the $0.34 per pound range.

About how much is the value of Karen's yearly turkey sales?

○ **A.** $12,000

○ **B.** $40,000

○ **C.** $60,000

○ **D.** $120,000

42   Which statement best describes a process that will determine Y, since V is unknown?

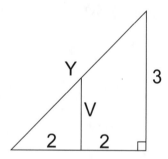

○ **A.** There is no process. Since V is unknown, Y cannot be determined.

○ **B.** V must also be 2, therefore Y will be 6.

○ **C.** Treat the small triangle as a separate problem, first finding its area, since V will be 3/4 or the larger height "3."

○ **D.** The larger triangle is a Pythagorean triple. V does not need to be known to solve for Y.

STOP

MATHEMATICS ASSESSMENT TWO—SESSION TWO SKILLS CHART

QUESTION	EALR. COMPONENT.GLE	ANSWER	KEYWORDS
22	ME04 1.2.6	see analysis	Estimate surface area of cylinders and prisms
23	NS05 1.1.8	D	Apply estimation strategies to determine reasonableness of results
24	GS02 1.3.4	A	Examine figures to determine symmetry
25	MC01 5.1.1	see analysis	Estimate derived units of measure
26	PS03 1.4.5	D	Analyze a model to determine appropriateness of a data set
27	PS03 1.4.6	C	Analyze or evaluate a statistical argument
28	AS03 1.5.6	A	Apply procedures to solve equations
29	SR01 2.1.1	see analysis	Analyze a situation to define a problem
30	SR01 2.1.2	C	Recognize when information is missing or is extraneous
31	GS01 1.3.1	C	Apply understanding of geometric properties
32	SR04 3.2.2	see analysis	Analyze information to draw conclusions
33	SR05 3.3.2	B	Analyze thinking and mathematical ideas
34	CU01 4.1.2	D; see analysis	Synthesize information for a given purpose
35	AS01 1.5.2	D	Analyze a pattern to write an equation or rule
36	CU02 4.2.2	A	Describe the location of points that satisfy given conditions
37	MC01 5.1.2	see analysis	Find the equation of a line in a variety of ways
38	ME02 1.2.3	B	Convert units of measure within systems
39	ME03 1.2.5	C	Use formulas to find the volume of a cylinder
40	ME04 1.2.6	B	Estimate derived units of measure
41	SR02 2.2.2	B	Analyze a situation to define a problem
42	MC01 5.1.2	D	Use different mathematical models in the same situation

MATHEMATICS ASSESSMENT TWO—SESSION TWO: ANSWER KEY

22 Karen is working on the labeling for a new kind of soft drink that her marketing company is helping to promote. The can will be 5.5 inches tall and have a radius of 1.75 inches. About how much space is available on the sides of this can for labeling the product? **Explain in detail** your work using words, numbers, and/or diagrams.
Analysis: The outside of the can is like a rectangular wraparound billboard to Karen and her marketing firm. Circumference of this basic cylinder is found using $C = \pi D$. First convert radius to diameter, then insert the values into the formula: 3.1415 x 3.5 inches = 10.99, or 11 inches. The area is then found by multiplying height by circumference: 5.5 inches x 11 inches = 60 square inches.

23 On a multiple-choice test, Kate glanced at the problem below and decided that the answer must be "about 3"; therefore, any answers outside that range could be eliminated. Using her strategy of estimation, which of the following could be ruled out as a reasonable answer for the problem?

2 ___ + 1/3 + 1/5 = ___

Analysis: Using Kate's strategy of estimating to eliminate wrong answer choices, 15/12, which is only slightly larger than 1, is too low to be correct. *Choice D is correct.*

24 A square measures 7 centimeters along a side. How many lines of symmetry could be drawn through such a square?
Analysis: Lines of symmetry may be drawn through the center vertically, through the center horizontally, and through each pair of opposite corners. *Choice A is correct.*

25 An art museum in New York gets about three million visitors per year. About how many visitors should the museum be prepared to receive per week? **Explain in detail** your work using words, numbers, and/or diagrams.
Analysis: The easiest way to answer this question is to use estimation. Estimate 50 weeks in the year. Divide 3,000,000 by 50, which equals 60,000. The museum should be prepared for about 60,000 visitors each week.

26 Jim started a new company 14 months ago recycling animal manure into useable fuels. Sales for his company have increased steadily since its founding. Jim has noticed that month-over-month sales appear to follow the pattern given below:

(previous month's sales) x 2 = next month's sales

The company's sales figures were plotted on a graph. Which of the following would **best** describe this data?
Analysis: The data is inconclusive about this company's sales, since the growth rate cannot be maintained at this level over a period of time. This can be more easily seen by taking sales data, perhaps using $100.00 for month 1, and plotting several months of data on a graph. *Choice D is correct.*

27 Rainfall was 0.5 inches on Monday, 0.75 inches on Tuesday, and 1.00 inches on Wednesday. On Friday, rainfall was 1.5 inches. Brian was away on Thursday and unable to measure the rainfall on that day, but he put in his journal for Thursday, "It rained 1.25 inches today." Which of the following **best** describes the accuracy of this entry?
Analysis: It corresponds to the recorded rainfall trend, but since the data is not known, no reasonable conclusion can be drawn. This is the nature of data missing within a set, or predicting events beyond known data points. In real-life terms, though, the odds are slim that exact, measured, and incremental increases in rainfall would occur over an uninterrupted five-day period. *Choice C is correct.*

28 Which of the following is the simplified $y = mx + b$ version of the equation $4x - 4 = 8y$?
Analysis: The equation is already close to being simplified. First factor out a 4: $4(x - 1) = 4(2y)$. This leaves $2y = x - 1$, which becomes $y = x/2 - 1/2$ or $y = 1/2x - 1/2$. *Choice A is correct.*

MATHEMATICS ASSESSMENT TWO—SESSION TWO: ANSWER KEY

29 On Monday, an oil company's stock rose from $108.00 to $110.16 on news that the company would receive special tax advantages. On Tuesday, the stock rose to $112.36 after being awarded a low-cost lease to drill on government lands. On Wednesday, the company announced that it would move some of its operations off-shore, thereby avoiding the payment of certain taxes; the stock closed up that day at $114.60. On Thursday, investors began buying the stock with renewed interest, and on that new volume it closed at $116.89. On Friday, it was announced that the government was exempting oil companies for responsibility in clean-ups related to chemical spills, and the stock again closed up, at $119.22. Over the weekend, it was announced by company representatives that they would no longer fund employee pension plans, thereby saving the company future expenses. What should the stock close at on Monday, if the stock price reacts in the same way it has to previous news? **Explain in detail** your thinking using words, numbers, and/or diagrams.
Analysis: Since this stock has increased by 2% each day, extending the pattern from the last known data point, $119.22, would yield a price of $121.60:
$119.22 x 1.02 = $121.60.

30 Corrine plans to paint a living room and a bedroom the same color of paint. The paint costs $21.99 per gallon, and a single gallon is enough to cover 2,200 square feet. She plans to apply two coats of paint in both rooms. The living room is exactly 1.5 times the size of the bedroom. The paint may also be purchased by the quart, at a cost of $11.99. The instructions on the back of the can state that a quart will only cover 500 square feet, which is not 25% of what the gallon can states as the coverage for a full gallon of paint. What information must still be known before a reasonable cost estimate for paint can be determined for this job?
Analysis: Since the living room is given as 1.5 times the size of the bedroom, only the size of the bedroom surfaces need to be known. The estimate, by nature, would not be so precise as to mathematically require a certain number of quarts, especially considering there will be 2 coats of paint and some likely amount of waste. Since a quart costs about half of what a gallon of paint does, it would be hard to justify buying a quart during the estimate stage anyway. The cost of other materials is not part of the question. *Choice C is correct.*

31 What is the cross-section of a three-dimensional figure?
Analysis: The cross-section of a three-dimensional figure must be another three-dimensional figure. *Choice C is correct.*

32 A rectangular prism with a height of 12 cm, a width of 12 cm, and a length of 20 cm will have the height expanded to 16 cm. About how much larger in percentage is the new figure? **Explain in detail** your work using words, numbers, and/or diagrams.
Analysis: The height of the prism is increased from 12 cm to 16 cm, or by 1/3. Therefore, the volume of the larger prism would be about 30% greater than the original prism. Another way to solve this problem would be to calculate the volume of each of the prisms and find the percentage of increase. The first prism had a volume of 2,880, which became 3,840 after the height was increased. The difference in volume, 960, divided by the volume of the smaller prism, will yield the percentage of increase in volume: 960 ÷ 2,880 = 0.33333, or about 30%.

33 A sausage maker guarantees that not less than 62.2% of its pork sausage is made of pork. Based only on this information, which of the following would be impossible to support? **Explain in detail** your thinking using words, numbers, and/or diagrams.
Analysis: It cannot logically be supported that the sausage must not have any grain or cereal filler in it, since the composition of the remaining 37.8% has not been revealed. *Choice B is correct.*

MATHEMATICS ASSESSMENT TWO—SESSION TWO: ANSWER KEY

34 Owen works for a jewelry manufacturing company that specializes in making gold jewelry. Over the past five years, Owen has tracked the price of gold, his company's total sales, and his company's profits.

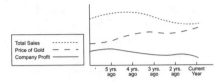

Which of the following statements has the least basis to be defended, based on the data shown? **Explain in detail** your thinking using words, numbers, and/or diagrams.
Analysis: The prediction that profits will rise once gold drops again cannot be supported since the declining profit may not be a factor of sales or gold prices. Factors such as poor management or unpopular jewelry designs may be the reason for the declining profits. *Choice D is correct.*

35 Russell developed a table to describe the amount of money that owed is depending on how many large pretzels a customer orders at his pretzel stand.

Number of Pretzels	Amount Owed
1	$0.89
2	$1.78
3	$2.57
4	$3.36
5	$4.05

Based on the information given, which of the following formulas would work for determining the purchase amount, A, regardless of the number of pretzels, P, ordered?
Analysis: Russell's pricing and discount structure appears to allow for discounts as more units are sold, but not enough data has been supplied to establish a pattern, or a formula derived from that pattern. *Choice D is correct.*

36 The point (1, 1) is an equidistant point for which of the following pairs of points?
Analysis: Making a rough sketch on a coordinate grid supplies a quick check. The point (1, 1) is an equidistant point for the pair of points, (-1, -1) and (3, 3). *Choice A is correct.*

37 What is the slope of the line that passes through the points (1, 2) and (5, 2)? **Explain in detail** your work using words, numbers, and/or diagrams.
Analysis: The line that passes through the points (1, 2) and (5, 2) is horizontal. A horizontal line has a slope of 0.

38 Which of the following is the equivalent of 1,075 centimeters?
Analysis: The equivalent of 1,075 centimeters is 10.75 meters, since centimeters ÷ by 100 yields meters: $1,075 \div 100 = 10.75$. *Choice B is correct.*

39 What is the volume of a cylinder that has a diameter of 10 inches and a height of 2.5 times that size?
Analysis: Use the standard formula for volume, $V = \pi r^2 h$. First, the diameter is twice the radius, so $V = \pi(5^2)h$. The problem gives the height as 2.5 times the diameter, which is 25. The formula will look like: $V = \pi(25)\ 25 = \pi 625 = 1,963.43$. *Choice C is correct.*

40 Kylie knows the drive to her grandmother's house usually takes about 5 hours, 45 minutes. Her grandmother's house is 288 miles from Kylie's house, but they'll actually be starting their trip from her aunt's house, which adds another sixteen miles to their trip. What kind of pace can Kylie expect on this trip if things go as they usually do?
Analysis: They have about 300 miles to travel in about 6 hours, so the pace they have should be about $300 \div 6$, or about 50 mph. The additional 16 miles does not affect the average speed of the trip. *Choice B is correct.*

MATHEMATICS ASSESSMENT TWO—SESSION TWO: ANSWER KEY

41 Every six or seven weeks, Karen's Turkey Farm is able to take 2,000 birds to market, each weighing about 8 pounds. The wholesale price of turkeys is usually in the $.34 per pound range. About how much is the value of Karen's yearly turkey sales?

Analysis: Turkeys going to market every six or seven weeks would mean about eight marketable loads of turkeys per year. Also, 2000 birds weighing about 8 pounds each is 16,000 pounds of turkeys. So Karen gets about 8 x 16,000 pounds, or 128,000 pounds of turkeys to market each year. At $0.34 per pound, the value of Karen's yearly turkey sales is about $43,520.00. *Choice B is correct.*

42 Which statement best describes a process that will determine Y, since V is unknown?

Analysis: Since the triangle is a 3-4-5, or a Pythagorean triple, V does not need to be known to solve for Y. *Choice D is correct.*

MATHEMATICS ASSESSMENT CORRELATION CHART

Use this chart to identify areas that need improvement for individual students or for the class as a whole. For example, enter students' names in the left-hand column. When a student misses a question, place an "X" in the corresponding box. A column with a large number of "Xs" shows that the class needs more practice with that particular indicator.

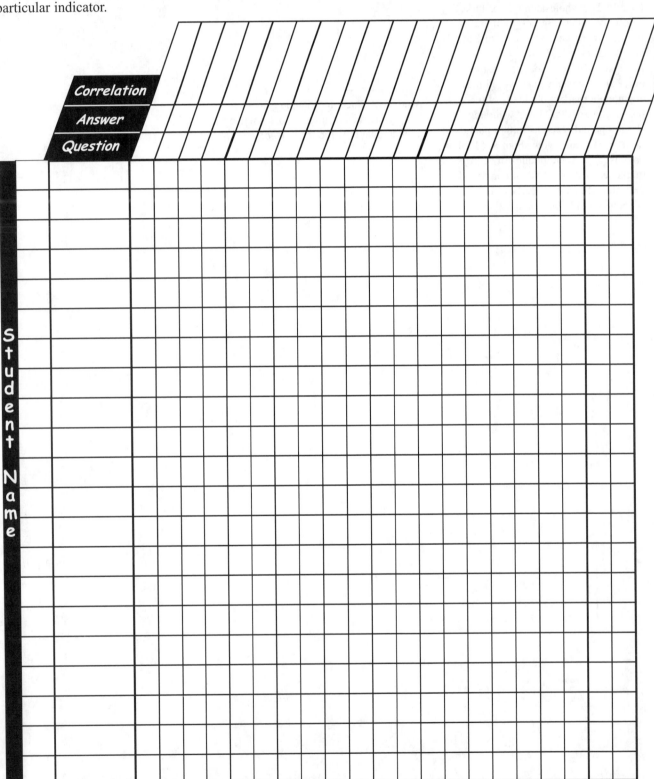

MATHEMATICS ASSESSMENT CORRELATION CHART

Use this chart to identify areas that need improvement for individual students or for the class as a whole. For example, enter students' names in the left-hand column. When a student misses a question, place an "X" in the corresponding box. A column with a large number of "Xs" shows that the class needs more practice with that particular indicator.

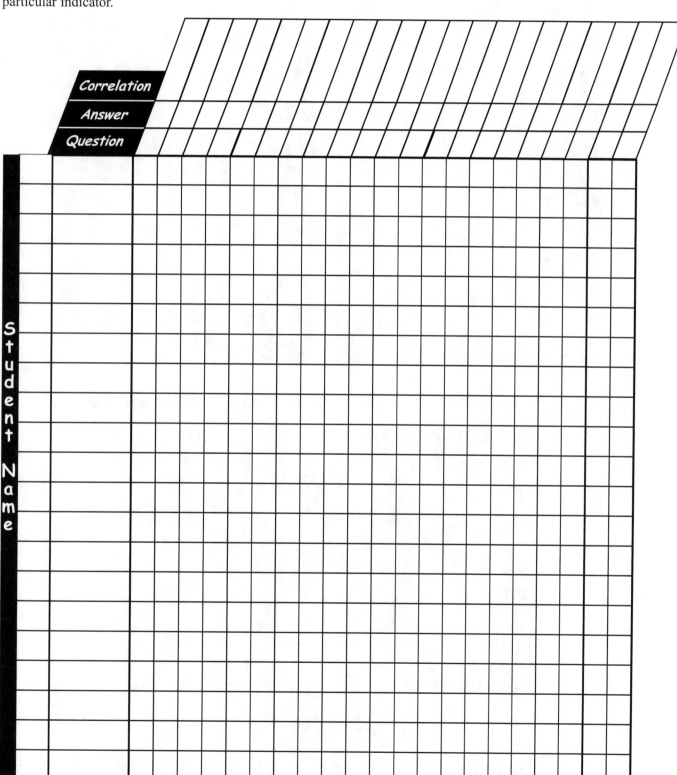

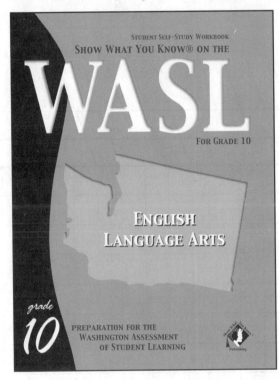

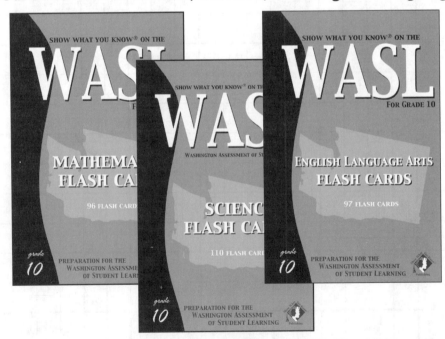